10663000

Response **A**bility **P**athways
Restoring Bonds of Respect

Response
Ability
Pathways

Restoring Bonds of Respect

Larry Brendtro and Lesley du Toit

Pretext, Cape Town

Response Ability Pathways
Restoring Bonds of Respect

© 2005 by Circle of Courage

All rights reserved including the reproduction
of this book in whole or part in any form.

A collaboration between:
Child and Youth Care Agency for Development, South Africa
Circle of Courage
No Disposable Kids at Starr Commonwealth

Children's art is reproduced from the journal
Reclaiming Children and Youth
Cover art is courtesy of CYCAD, South Africa

ISBN 978-0-9584770-9-3

International Edition

www.pretext.co.za

Contents

Acknowledgements

Response Ability Pathways [RAP] was inspired by many persons and organizations committed to reclaiming all of our children and youth. RAP uses the Circle of Courage model described by Larry Brendtro, Martin Brokenleg, and Steve Van Bockern in *Reclaiming Youth at Risk*. That book spawned the non-profit research and training organization, Reclaiming Youth International [RYI].

Those who have assisted us in the design of RAP include the North American team of Martin Brokenleg, Steve Van Bockern, Martin Mitchell, Herm McCall, Mark Freado, Scott Larson, Edna Olive, and J. C. Chambers. In South Africa the team includes Charles Coetzee, Nico Els, and Jacqui Michael. Youth consultants were Tim Els and Mpho Mofekeng. Assisting in editorial and publishing activities were Brian Gannon and Janna Brendtro. We extend our appreciation to the young people whose art is included in these pages.

Our work is enriched by many colleagues from around the world including James Anglin, Sibylle Artz, Howard Bath, Randolph Boardman, Diana Boswell, Waln Brown, Jack Calhoun, Nancy Carlsson-Paige, Richard Curwin, Coenie du Toit, Frank Fecser, Minister Geraldine Fraser-Moleketi, Barbara Huff, Judge Ernestine Gray, Lili Garfinkel, John Hoover, Terry Hood, Cathann Kress, Linda Lantieri, Erik Laursen, Nicholas Long, James Longhurst, Ken McCluskey, Jennifer McEldowney, Arlin Ness, Reggie Newkirk, Polly Nichols, Constance Quirk, Father Chris Riley, Advocate Ann Skelton, John Seita, Mary Shahbazian, Tom Tate, André Viviers, Mary Wood, and other colleagues from RYI and NACCW.

We dedicate this book to those young people who daily face difficult challenges in their life journeys. John Seita, a former troubled child who is now an expert on resilience, poses this challenge: "No longer should we expect children to navigate without a map, steer without a rudder, or seek without a friend." RAP provides tools to support all young persons as they travel pathways toward responsibility.

Foreword

Martin Brokenleg

In my childhood, I knew Lakota elders who were at the Battle of the Little Big Horn when Custer was killed. My grandfather was 50 years old when he first saw white people. He was a medicine man and a horse trainer who gave us our family name, Brokenleg.

My mother and father both were stolen from the embrace of their family and sent to residential schools. There they were treated as inferiors to be trained rather than sacred ones to be loved. Because they were so repulsed by these experiences, Mother and Father made certain we were raised according to our traditional Lakota tribal ways.

My earliest memories are joyful ones – full of warmth, laughter, emotional connectedness, and many, many people – all of whom deeply cared about me. Although we were poor in possessions, we were rich in personal relationships because of love and constant support. My many uncles were my fathers and my aunts were my mothers. Dozens of grandmothers and grandfathers told me of our traditions and kindly scolded me if I strayed from these cultural teachings.

I experienced the many relatives I have and felt *belonging* with them all. My relatives included not only people but animals, plants, stars, the wind, and those from the spirit world. I was to walk gently and, by learning well, would know *mastery* over my life. Frequently, I was cautioned to use wisely the power which made me *independent*. I could be a blessing or a problem just by my behavior. Under all circumstances, I was to know that *generosity* would require work and selflessness, but it was always the right response.

Today, I live more with the memory of my relatives and ancestors than their presence. I am now a man who sees old age on the horizon. I can also see the great and frequent pain our children live with, no matter where they are in the world.

Families today have many distractions that take attention away from our children. The struggle to earn a living and provide for children may require parents to spend less time with those they love. An increasing proportion of young people know the hollow emptiness of loneliness, the searing suffering of pain and loss, the icy silence of abandonment whether physical or emotional.

These children in pain are blessed if they have caring adults in their lives.

One of the most difficult transitions to achieve is the shift from an idea to the implementation of that idea. However important a goal might be, getting that goal to happen is the problem. Something in us resists change even if we need that change. As one who has spent at least half my life on diets, I know how difficult lasting change can be.

In our writing about the "Circle of Courage" Larry Brendtro, Steve Van Bockern, and I brought together different racial backgrounds and upbringing. The Circle of Courage philosophy is universal, although we initially used Lakota images and stories to express the ideas. Because these values are universal, we have found broad acceptance from those who care deeply about children and youth in many parts of the world.

The Lakota leader Sitting Bull once told some white people, "Let us put our minds together and see what kind of life we can make for our children." This book and the associated RAP training program do just that. We are encouraged to put our minds together to lead our children on pathways to responsibility.

All children need loving, caring, committed, and consistent adults around them, if they are to bloom fully. We must become the extended family of elders and parents who once surrounded every child. We may not be parents by blood, but we are the child's parent by love, caring, and dedication.

As you study this book think about what it teaches and implies. Then, experience the RAP training to apply the Circle of Courage principles to the lives of children. You will awaken to the strength of spirit that is the birthright of every child. You will see the promises of successful and joyous living that you can inspire in children. You will know the deep satisfaction of trusting connections with young persons as they discover a new life pathway. As Black Elk said,

"If you think about it, you will see that it is true."

The Rev. Canon Dr. Martin Brokenleg is a psychologist, director of the Native Ministries Programme, and professor of First Nations Ministry & Theology at the Vancouver School of Theology, University of British Columbia, Canada.

Introduction

Everything should be made as simple as possible but not simpler.
— Albert Einstein

Einstein proposed using down-to-earth vocabulary so key ideas in any field could be understood by everyone. This book translates research on positive child development into practical methods to foster pathways to responsibility. This text is written in practical language with footnotes documenting the research base behind the RAP methods.[1]

Response Ability Pathways – or RAP – is a training course for youth professionals, educators, parents, and other adult or peer mentors.[2] All who are concerned with young people need the ability to respond to their needs rather than react to their problems. RAP teaches skills to connect with kids in need, clarify problems, and restore bonds. Following Circle of Courage resilience principles, RAP addresses needs for belonging, mastery, independence, and generosity.[3]

Children are like acorns with the potential to become great oaks.[4] All are endowed with the seeds of some unique "genius." But as they struggle and grow, they encounter many challenges and make missteps:

- Albert Einstein and Thomas Edison were terrible students who hated school.
- As a boy, Ghandi was thin, sickly, and frightened. His courageous stand against oppression in South Africa and India challenged colonial powers.
- Polar explorer, Robert Perry, was the only child of a widow and clung closely to his mother to escape neighbourhood boys who bullied him about his cowardice.
- As a girl, Eleanor Roosevelt was sullen, friendless, and fought teachers. But she dreamed of one day helping those less fortunate. She would realise her goals as wife of a president and winner of the Nobel Peace Prize.

The folk tales of every culture recount "the power of one" to triumph over personal hardship and make a difference in the lives of others.[5] Cervantes once said, *great persons are able to do great kindnesses*. Even those from very different backgrounds have inner strengths and can become responsible contributors to the human community.

1

A Portrait of Pain

I didn't want no one to love any more.
I had been hurt too many times.
– Richard Cardinal[6]

Richard Cardinal was a First Nations boy from Canada who was removed from his alcoholic parents at age four. He and his siblings were placed with different White foster families throughout the province of Alberta. Over the next thirteen years, Richard would learn much about pain as he was shuttled through many foster settings, group homes, children's shelters, and locked facilities. Cut off from his family and cultural roots, Richard's most basic physical, emotional, and growth needs were frustrated.

Richard communicated his pain in the language of troubling behaviour and self-destructive acts. Angry adults reacted with increased punishment and rejection. When Richard wet his bed, he was shamed and humiliated by being stripped naked and beaten cruelly before an audience of other foster children. When he broke rules, he was starved and given a sack of raw turnips for food. His longest placement was four years confined to a dingy basement where he had to walk on planks to avoid the water covering the floor.

As he approached adolescence, Richard was again in and out of different placements and schools. Richard's talents went untapped, and he failed all of his subjects. He showed more interest in physical work, caring for farm animals, but this still left him empty of human love. In desperate attempts to control the course of his life, Richard repeatedly tried to run away. He would head to the north, once making it as far as the village where he first lived as a small child.

Facing repeated rejection and pain, Richard continued on the pathway of problems. One foster parent found a diary Richard had been keeping and was shocked to read about how much anger he expressed because he seldom showed this outwardly. On isolated occasions Richard acted out, but not directly against persons: he stole a truck and shot a cow. Mostly Richard directed his rage inward. Lonely and depressed, Richard called attention to his pain with self-destructive acts. He cut his wrists once while in school and again while sitting on the street in front of a convenience store, bleeding onto the sidewalk. Another time he was found curled up in a doghouse, wih self-inflicted wounds and "please help me" written in his own blood. Crying out for help which did not come, Richard was losing the will to live.

Occasional interventions by treatment professionals failed to address Richard's needs. Richard tried to drown his pain in drink and again attempted suicide. He was brought by ambulance to a hospital and nearly died. He woke up strapped to a restraint table and cried out in pain. A nurse responded by releasing Richard's bonds and embracing him, assuring him that everything would be all right. He could not remember how long it had been since someone had hugged him as he missed it very much. He was discharged the next day without any restorative plan.

Richard died spiritually long before he took his own life. He was found hanging from a birch tree in the back yard of his last foster home. He left behind his diary describing his years of struggle and suffering. Richard's voice was finally heard, as his words provided a window into his private world. His life story was documented by the National Film Board of Canada[7] in an award-winning video. It is a testament to failure of approaches that only react to surface problems but fail to reach the inside kid. Richard wrote these lines when told he had to leave yet another foster home where he had lived for a time with his brother:

I had four hours before I would leave my family and friends behind. I went into the bedroom and dug out my old harmonica. I went down to the barn-yard and sat on the fence. I began to play real slow and sad-like for the occasion, but halfway through the song my lower lip began to quiver and I knew I was going to cry. And I was glad so I didn't even try to stop myself. I guess that my foster mother heard me and must have

come down to comfort me. When she put her arm around me, I pulled away and ran up the roadway. I didn't want no one to love any more. I had been hurt too many times. So I began to learn the art of blocking out all emotions and shut out the rest of the world. The door would open to no one.
Love can be gentle as a lamb or ferocious as a lion. It is something to be welcomed; it is something to be afraid of. It is good and bad, yet people live, fight, die for this. Somehow people can cope with it. I don't know. I think I would not be happy with it, yet I am depressed and sad without it. Love is very strange.

Richard's final diary entry is an apology for the pain he might cause others by his suicide. In a final gesture of generosity, he shares his love for his brother and then tells persons in his life not to take his death personally, "I just can't take any more."

Pain, Lots of Pain

Children encounter many difficulties growing up in this unsettled world. Most are able to steer clear of the more serious hazards to positive development. Those not so fortunate are physically or psychologically battered about in hostile and turbulent environments. Swimming in rivers of pain, they struggle to survive using whatever means they know.[8]

While our hearts go out to children who hurt, when their behaviour troubles others, concern can quickly turn to blame. Such youngsters are given negative labels like disruptive, disordered, and disturbed. Many seriously troubled kids are treated as damaged goods to be discarded. Their troubled behaviour is a cry of pain, a call for help that often goes unheard.[9]

In his book *Pain, Lots of Pain,* Brian Raychaba shines a light into the little known inner world of troubled young persons.[10] He interviewed Canadian youth who had been removed from their families. Raychaba himself came from such a background, so most quickly opened up to him. They recounted the powerlessness of being at the mercy of traumatic life events. They believed their pain was seldom understood, even by trained professionals. Yet, beneath their fury or fear, most hungered for love and hoped for a better future.

3

In a study of youth at risk in ten treatment programs, James Anglin of the University of Victoria in British Columbia concluded that *each of these young persons without exception* experiences deep and pervasive emotional pain.[11] But few who work with such children are trained to recognise or address the pain concealed beneath the problem behaviour. Instead, the typical discipline intervention is a sharp verbal reprimand (e.g., "Watch your language!") or threatening consequences or loss of privileges. Anglin concluded that many who deal with difficult youngsters *react* to their own frustration, rather than *respond* to the pain and needs of the young person. This is the key distinction between ineffective and effective discipline.

Human behaviour is motivated by feelings of pain or pleasure. Before children are even able to speak, they can experience a full range of emotions from "lung-wrenching anger to limb-flapping joy."[12] By eighteen months, children have developed the capacity to "size up a new acquaintance as friendly or threatening, respectful or humiliating, supportive or undermining," in order to behave accordingly.[13] By school-age, they can also detect a full range of positive and negative emotions in others.[14]

While children quickly acquire the universal language of emotions, it takes many years to learn to intelligently manage these feelings. A small child in emotional pain instinctively displays tears or distress. Ideally, caregivers *respond* to the child's pain with empathy and try to meet the child's needs. However, sometimes a youngster's behaviour stirs up such distress in us that we *react* emotionally and give back the pain.

Some problem behaviours are reactions to a temporary stressful situation. Others trace back to earlier trauma or mistreatment. A girl describes her pathway from being hurt to hurting others:

After my dad assaulted me when I was eight, I was put in a foster home. I was there for a year and a half. That was the first time the violence really came out of me.

This small girl, abused and removed from her family, probably had painful feelings of anger and depression, painful thoughts that she was bad and unworthy of love, and reacted by hurting others. Pain is a powerful force engulfing emotions, thoughts, and behaviour. For example:

4

- *Painful emotions* include negative inner states such as fear, anger, sadness, and shame. There are dozens of names for bad feelings but most are variations of a handful of basic emotions.
- *Painful thoughts* include worry, distrust, hatred, guilt, and helplessness. Defence mechanisms like denial, blame, and rationalization distort thinking in order to suppress painful feelings.
- *Pain-based behaviour* is a reaction to painful emotions and thinking. A person may try to escape from pain, act out pain, relive pain, block out pain, cause pain to others, or even punish themselves with more pain.

Those who cannot constructively cope with problems often turn to defensive *fight and flight* behaviour. Returning to the story of Richard Cardinal, we can see numerous examples of self-defeating reactions to distress:

- Preventing the pain of rejection by refusing to love again.
- Avoiding the pain of failure by abandoning attempts to succeed.
- Escaping the pain of powerlessness by running away.
- Internalising the pain of anger by self-destructive acts.
- Medicating the pain of loneliness with alcohol and other drugs.
- Brooding on the pain of hopelessness in withdrawal and depression.

Rather than hurting others, Richard Cardinal turned his problems inward. Many children act out their pain and create problems for others. They react to powerlessness with defiance and rebellion. They repay the pain of victimisation by victimising others through meanness, bullying, and retribution. They mask the pain of emptiness through the wild pursuit of pleasure. And they silence the pain of conscience by tricking themselves with selfish and calloused thinking.

Whether young people show pain by hurting themselves or others, flight and fight reactions only make matters worse. These are emergency pain-avoidance measures but do not provide real solutions.[15] They fail to heal pain, meet needs, or develop strengths. Humans are by nature problem-solvers who try out various strategies to cope with challenges and difficulties. When their attempts are adaptive, they lead to social harmony and personal well-being. But when they cannot cope, their pain-driven reactions lead to destructive and self-defeating behaviour.

Tit for Tat

Our human brains are hard-wired to react to others in the way they react to us. Like a mirror image, friendliness usually invites friendliness while hostility sparks hostility. Psychologists call this the "Tit for Tat" rule. The principle is very simple:

- *On the first encounter with another person, be friendly.*
- *Then, return the friendly or hostile reaction encountered.* [16]

Humans by nature seek out social connections. Tit for Tat offers a starting point for recruiting friends. But a friendly nature could make one vulnerable to those with hostile intentions. Thus, humans also have an inbuilt self-protective option. At the first sign of danger or disrespect, we are programmed to stop being friendly and display hostile or defensive behaviour.

Tit for Tat worked well when humans lived in simpler societies. It provided a better way for dealing with strangers than treating each outsider as an enemy. Tit for Tat still operates across all cultures and is probably embedded in the human genetic code. But in impersonal, high-stress cultures, we are surrounded by strangers. Tit for Tat is too limiting as tense encounters can easily escalate into violence. Tit for Tat is also morally self-centred. The Tit for Tat rule is a payback scheme while the Golden Rule calls for treating others the way we would like to be treated.

Tit for Tat is a poor strategy for parenting, teaching, or treatment. Love and hate reactions are inevitable with children showing emotional problems.[17] The challenge is to prevent a vicious cycle where hate is answered with hate.

Children in pain are likely to draw adults into escalating Tit for Tat hostility. They telegraph pain and are hypersensitive to the most subtle signs of disrespect. Since angry conflict can ruin relationships and even lead to violence, both youth and adults need to learn ways to creatively resolve conflict. Successful coping is a "double struggle" as we try to manage both the external difficulty and our internal emotional reactions.[18]

One of the most amazing findings from brain research is the role of the amygdala, which is the command centre of the emotional brain. *Amygdala* is the Greek word for almond, and the brain has two of these almond shaped structures. Like radar, the amygdala scans incoming stimuli searching for possible pain or pleasure.[19]

When signs of threat or opportunity are detected, positive or negative emotions are triggered.

The amygdala is not only on the lookout for *physical* pain or pleasure, but *social* pain or pleasure as well. Humans need to know if they should approach or avoid one another. In any personal encounter, the amygdala makes instant judgments about whether the individual poses a danger or an opportunity.

Emotionally charged events are recorded into long-term memory. Thus we are more likely to recall painful or pleasurable experiences.[20] This is why even brief stressful or exciting events can be remembered for a lifetime.

Describing troubled emotions as "pain" is more than a figure of speech. When we say we have "hurt feelings," this is literally true. Researchers found that physical and social pain operate in similar ways in the brain.[21] Brain scans show that being excluded or rejected triggers feelings of distress and a burst of activity in the area of the brain registers physical pain.[22] Students who were best able to handle rejection had greater activity in the higher brain. Being able to think about or verbalise distress may calm the emotional brain. This may be why telling stories to a therapist and expressing feelings in poems and diaries is helpful.

Humans are highly sensitive to rejection because social bonds are crucial for survival.[23] Thus, humans have a brain-based warning system that is activated at any sign one is being excluded so the person can take corrective action. When signs of rejection are registered, this triggers the emotion of shame.[24] Shame is a highly painful emotion that attacks self-worth. In contrast, belonging produces feelings of pride and well-being.[25]

Shame is often confused with guilt. Guilt focuses on behaviour and can motivate one to make amends.[26] The pain of shame can be so intense that it leads to destructive acts against self or others. Rejected persons who do not find substitute belongings become social outcasts. In the extreme, shame can lead to suicide, or the person turns pain outward and attacks those seen as causing the pain of rejection. The quiet, bullied student who shoots his tormentors and then himself is an example of shame directed both at self and others.

While shame is universal, culture influences how people react. In some Native American and Asian groups, suicide was once an acceptable response to the shame of loss of love or defeat in battle. In aggression-prone cultures, like the Celtic traditions that shaped the American South, any insult or show of disrespect led to a duel in the belief that one cannot "lose face" without striking back.[27]

Youth excluded from a group often switch their allegiance to other peers in order to replace the pain of shame with the pride of belonging. Kids who fail in school and are rejected by their peers have very low self-worth. But if they join a gang or group of other social outcasts, tested self-esteem actually increases!

Children who have experienced much hostility do not get used to it. Instead they are on guard for the slightest sign of disrespect.[28] If they feel they are being violated, it may seem logical to them to be violent in return. An abused youth describes this reaction to physical discipline:

> **If you put your hands on me – I'm breaking your neck, you know what I mean? A few people grabbed me and tried to put me in my room and I just smashed them…. I've been grabbed all my life. You know what I mean? It just turns me right off when someone touches me.[29]**

Angry conflicts are highly interactive.[30] Once "Tit for Tat" programs are triggered, conflict is self-perpetuating until one party disengages or is defeated. Sometimes the conflict continues to stir long after the event as a young person becomes a prisoner of hate.[31]

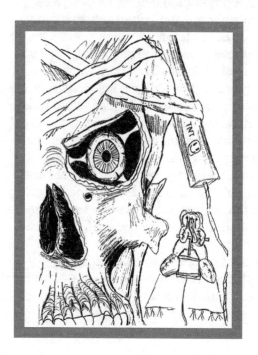

Causing Others Pain

Hurt people hurt people.
– Native American Proverb

Humans are born with the ability to feel empathy with persons in pain. So, why would they get satisfaction by causing harm? As it turns out, our negative thoughts and feelings block empathy. For example, we excuse our own mistakes and blame others. This self-centred thinking allows us to tune out the hurt of others.[32] We are most susceptible to thinking errors when emotionally aroused and when we are under the influence of a powerful group or authority figure. At such moments, the brain switches from logical control to control by others.

When one "goes along" with others, individual decision making is turned off.[33] If those in charge are positive, cooperation is healthy. If the group or leader is destructive, individuals are easily misled to model this behaviour as well. Since children do not have well-developed logical brain controls over emotions, they are more susceptible to the excitement of the moment and group pressure through emotional contagion. Even adults in times of threat suspend logical thinking and rush to embrace a powerful leader or group. Our natural desire for cooperation causes us to give up self-control by *obedience* to authority and *conformity* to a group.

Violence thrives in cultures of coercion.[34] In such settings, distorted group thinking silences conscience and individuals no longer take personal responsibility for their actions.[35] In an astounding experiment, Stanford University psychologists recruited normal mentally healthy college students to role play either guards or inmates in a simulated prison experiment. In a short period of time, the guards became abusive and the prisoners were either compliant or rebellious. All manner of abuse, humiliation, and punishment was administered. Prisoners were deprived of most basic needs, stripped naked, marched around with bags covering their heads, and brought to the edge of mental breakdown. The experiment had to be cancelled after a week because those who wielded absolute authority became highly abusive.[36]

Violent kids who react from fear or group contagion may not immediately show remorse.[37] This doesn't mean they are "bad kids" or "kids without conscience." Those who really get to know such kids seldom find them truly empty. After studying aggressive children for half a century, Fritz Redl said he had never met a kid who was truly a psychopath. However, children not bonded to adults have delays in conscience development. They show little concern for others and can act in cruel ways. In Tit for Tat fashion, hurt children have few qualms about hurting others.

The pathway to violence usually starts with mistreatment or trauma in the early life of the child. Kids who cannot cope with severe emotional pain are in a state of crisis. Those who brood about a problem may decide either to turn anger inward or to act out. Once they become comfortable hurting others, change is more difficult. Without positive social bonds, such persons continue to be a danger to others.[38]

Many children are deeply hurt by mistreatment, racism, sexism, religious bigotry, and hostility based on sexual orientation.[39] For those who work with children in pain, it is often self-protective to avoid or attack their problem behaviour. This reaction can only be overridden through a belief in the potential strengths of every youth.

Drowning in Distress

The starting point for all problems is stress, a state of physical and psychological arousal that signals some challenge or difficulty.[40] Stressful events make up the fabric of normal life. But stress that becomes too intense and lasting leads to pain-based behaviour. Hundreds of stressors surround children:

- *Physical stressors* disrupt well-being. These include abuse, illness, hunger, lack of sleep, noise, crowding, and dangerous environments.
- *Emotional stressors* produce psychological pain as experienced in feelings of fear, anger, grief, shame, guilt, and worthlessness.
- *Social stressors* disrupt normal growth needs. These impede the development of belonging, mastery, independence, and generosity.

Stress in the family interferes with parenting and weakens adult-child bonds. This includes frequent moves, lack of supportive relatives, divorce, solo parenting, death of a caregiver, harried work schedules, inadequate child care, substance abuse, and neglect. School stressors, such as the fear of failure, disrupt

11

learning. Peer relationships are often problematic during adolescence. Mismatches of temperament between children and caregivers and intrusive discipline strategies can also increase stress.[41] When basic needs are frustrated, children experience chronic stress.

A study of students in an inner city alternative school during one school year demonstrated that most were experiencing massive stress in their lives.[42] All experienced or witnessed violence in school. Many came from stressful or abusive families or were even homeless at times. Conflicts with peers were frequent and frightening. These stressors seriously hampered their ability to perform in school. But school personnel were seldom aware of most student crises, although they daily dealt with the behavioural fallout from such stress.

Children overwhelmed by stress are in a state of ongoing crisis. While crisis is disruptive, it also can lead to potential opportunities. Crisis can motivate change. Humans in crisis instinctively reach out for the support of trusted persons. At such times, they are more open to influence from others. Managed correctly, crisis can provide powerful teaching moments. Managed ineptly, stress intensifies conflict and pain for all involved.

Most emotional and behavioural problems of children stem from the inability to cope with stress. Such stress can produce both inner emotional disturbance and outward social maladjustment.[43] This is why many youth show multiple problems such as depression, defiance, school failure, delinquency, substance abuse, and other risk-taking behaviours.[44] Acting out behaviour often masks inner emotional distress. A major study of delinquents found that over ninety percent showed clear evidence of "having been very unhappy or discontented in their life circumstances or extremely disturbed because of emotion-provoking situations or experiences."[45]

Children who are drowning in distress follow different pathways. Some act out in ways that invoke hostility from others. They get into conflicts with peers and contests with authority.[46] Others retreat into an inner world cut off from those who might offer support. But, however they show their pain, these are children of discouragement.

Overcoming Discouragement

For positive development, children must have their physical, emotional, and growth needs met by caring adults. Pain-based behaviour signals that some need is not being fulfilled.[47] We see this in the story of Richard Cardinal which began this chapter. Richard's *physical needs* were neglected. He was harshly beaten, deprived of food, kept in substandard surroundings, and in times of greatest pain was locked in settings using restraint and seclusion. Richard's *emotional needs* went unmet as he was cut off from his family and culture and placed with adults who treated him with intimidation and rejection. Richard was also deprived of normal *growth needs*, those experiences that enable children to build trusting relationships and develop potentials.

When growth needs are met, children can turn risk into resilience. Long before the terms *risk* and *resilience* came into common use, Alfred Adler used *courage* and *discouragement* to express similar ideas.[48] Courage is needed to surmount life's difficulties – but courage only comes from experiencing adversity.[49] Children need people in their lives who help them gain the courage to face difficulties without becoming overwhelmed and discouraged.

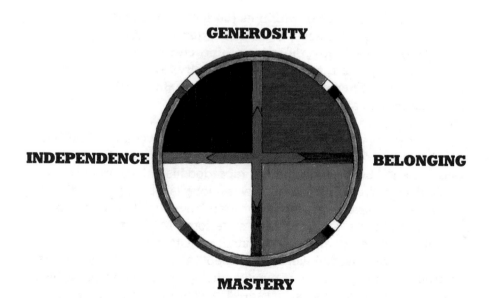

How do children develop courage and resilience? The answer is portrayed in the four directions of the Circle of Courage drawn by Lakota artist George Bluebird.[50] Beginning in the east, all children need to belong, to master, to become independent, and to contribute to others in a spirit of generosity.

Similar practices have existed in other cultures that deeply value children. Long before modern psychology, tribal people on many continents possessed sophisticated child-development knowledge. Passed on through oral traditions and careful modelling, elders taught important values to each new generation. In close kinship communities, such as tribes of Africa, Australasia, and the Americas, children were deeply respected and surrounded by caring relatives who nurtured their needs.

Pediatrician T. Berry Brazelton describes a child birth in a South American tribe. This was a peak event as a small crowd gathered to welcome their newest relative to the tribal circle. Those in attendance became "birth parents" who were allowed to share in raising this child. This tradition is unique but respect for children characterizes indigenous cultures worldwide. The Lakota (Sioux) term for child literally means *sacred being.* In the Maori tongue, a child is called *gift of the gods.* Indigenous Australians speak to children with great respect. Traditional African values concerning children are described by Zulu sociologist, Vilakazi:

A child draws from within us the inclination and instinct for kindness, gentleness, generosity, and love. Accordingly, there is nothing more revolting to our humanity than cruelty to children. These truths we knew at one time and, somehow, subsequently forgot.[51]

There is evidence that values of respect between children and adults were once part of the early tribal history on the European continent.[52] But throughout most recorded history, the treatment of children in Western civilization was a long tale of neglect and abuse.[53] Children were legally property to be used, misused, or discarded at the whims of their "superiors." Many believed children were evil and needed harsh punishment.

As Europeans conquered tribal people on many continents, they brought along practices of punitive discipline. The goal of colonial education was to "civilise savages" as children were ripped from their families and sent to distant residential schools. Youngsters who had never known hostility from elders were beaten harshly, even for speaking in their tribal tongue. A Native American recalls his forced removal to a church-sponsored institution as *the aboriginal sin.*[54] Indigenous Australians recall the cultural kidnapping of their children as *the stolen generation.*[55]

Child-rearing customs differ based on cultural values, but the basic needs of children have always been the same. Philosopher Mortimer Adler observed that not all values are relative, for absolute values are tied to *universal human needs.* [56] By this standard, the Circle of Courage is universal, for it is grounded in what Abraham Maslow called *growth needs.*[57] When these needs go unmet, children cannot develop their full potential, and they display a host of pain-based behaviours. Stated simply:

- *When growth needs are met, youth have positive outcomes.*
- *When growth needs are frustrated, youth show problems.*

Environments that fail to provide belonging, mastery, independence, and generosity cause great pain to children and are toxic to positive development. This was the tragedy of Richard Cardinal. Starving for love, Richard was cut off from human belonging. Though bright and creative, he found no outlet for mastery. Powerless to control his life, he could not develop responsible independence. Generous in the spirit of his Native tribal culture, he had no opportunity to be of value to others. Richard Cardinal was stripped of his birthright and his spirit was crushed.

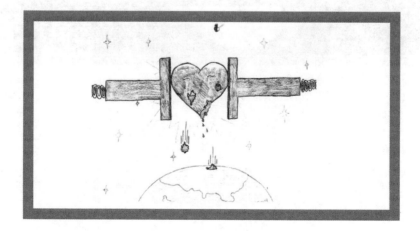

2

Fighting Pain with Pain

I have always believed it is our responsibility as adults to give children futures worth having. I have often been shocked and angered to see how shamefully we have failed in this responsibility.
— Graça Machel [58]

Punishment as Pain

Young people in conflict are reacting to physical, social, or emotional pain. How ironic that the principal means of managing problem behaviour has been to administer physical, social, or emotional pain. Einstein observed that common sense is the collection of prejudices acquired by age eighteen. This seems to apply to folk theories about punishment which continue in spite of all evidence about their ineffectiveness.

The word punishment comes from the Latin word *poèna,* which means "pain." To punish is to cause pain in reaction to undesired behaviour. To preserve social order, all societies have penalties for serious infractions. But such punishment will not necessarily eliminate problems. Often, punishing troubled children teaches them to become sneakier, fight adults, or wallow in self-blame.

Sociologists contend that whatever the intellectual rationalisation, punishment is first and foremost an instinctive, emotional reaction to threat. [59] Punishment can serve a useful function by defining standards necessary for social harmony. But the human instinct to punish is easily driven to excess. As Western culture embraced democratic values, punishment became more

17

civilised, for example, by replacing maiming with incarceration. Punishment may change its form but not its substance. Humans react defensively to perceived threat, and punishment attacks the supposed threat.

Dominator cultures operate under the threat of punishment.[60] The principle is very simple: "Do what I say or I will inflict pain." Many assume that coercion is necessary to avoid chaos. In fact, there is another more powerful method of social control. *Cultures of respect* create order through social bonds and restore harmony if people are hurt. This "restorative justice" ethic has operated for thousands of years in tribal cultures world-wide. A person who offends is made aware of how this behaviour hurt others and is allowed to make amends. Taking responsibility restores bonds of respect.[61]

Yet obedience training and impersonal "curriculums of control" have been the dominant ways of dealing with challenging children and youth.[62] We assume these coercive approaches are necessary, and we minimise the harmful effects of punishment. In fact, the term punishment is often sanitised with labels like "administering consequences" or "teaching them a lesson." It sounds uncivilised to say that we are inflicting pain to try to change behaviour.

In spite of attempts to eliminate harsh punishment, the coercive mindset persists. Thus, when South Africa became a democracy, corporal punishment was prohibited in schools and residential care settings. Many staff felt their authority was being undermined since they had no means of controlling problem behaviour. In similar situations across the world, staff simply found other ways to punish and control children. Prominent examples include expulsion and physical restraint which are now common in programs for challenging children and youth, even in some preschools!

Adults who feel threatened are biologically primed to strike back.[63] Even those trained for work with troubled youth may believe that coercive methods are a necessary evil in disciplining those who do not respond to usual behaviour management systems.[64] Coercion begins with verbal confrontation and threats. If these methods do not work, interventions escalate to physical restraint and removal. Few believe that coercion promotes educational growth; they just need more potent means to maintain order and authority in the face of difficult behaviour.

A threatened public often supports harsh treatment of troubled young people. In the United States, as youth crime dropped to the lowest levels in decades, fear of crime was hyped by politicians and the media. Schools adopted zero-tolerance policies to exclude disruptive students. The juvenile justice system built youth prisons and "boot camps" to teach respect. Such methods are even used in profitable private centres for troubled children. Desperate parents expend huge sums to have their troubled teen spirited off in the dead of the night by "escorts" to be held virtually incommunicado in remote "behaviour modification" camps described as Gulags.[65]

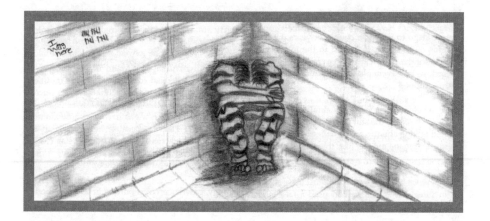

COERCIVE
vs
RESTORATIVE CLIMATES

Physical Coercion
- Punishment
- Deprivation
- Restraint

Physical Support
- Protection
- Nurturance
- Freedom

Emotional Coercion
- Threat
- Hostility
- Blame

Emotional Support
- Trust
- Respect
- Understanding

Social Coercion
- Exclusion
- Frustration
- Domination
- Unconcern

Social Support
- Belonging
- Mastery
- Independence
- Generosity

© 2004 Circle of Courage

Children instinctually resent coercion and force which includes all varieties of physical and psychological punishment.[66] The founder of modern behaviour modification, B.F. Skinner, concluded that punishment is a failed educational method.[67] More recently, many experts on education, mental health, and justice have called for ending highly coercive behaviour management with troubled children. But coercion thrives encoded in formal rules such as suspension and expulsion policies. Often coercion goes "underground" as those in power dish out punishments according to their own folk psychology of justice. The most widespread examples of coercion are subtle moment-by-moment human interactions that convey emotional negativity.

Coercive methods are common in settings for young people who present challenging behaviour. Behaviour management tactics range from mild restrictions to outright abuse. This does not suggest that all use of force is destructive. However, punitive behaviour management interferes with positive development. The accompanying table compares coercive versus restorative or supportive approaches. *Physical, emotional,* and *social coercion* are contrasted with methods providing *physical, emotional,* and *social support.* Specific examples are discussed in the following section.[68]

Physical Coercion

Physical coercion produces physiological distress. This involves physical punishment, deprivation, and restraint. In contrast, physical support fosters protection, nurturance, and freedom.

Punishment versus Protection

Children develop best in environments free from the fear of physical distress or harm. But, many coercive methods are intended to cause bodily pain. Beyond physical or sexual abuse, "corporal punishment" involves spanking, hitting, slamming, slapping, hair pulling, pressure points, and other painful treatment. Punishment by proxy uses peers to administer pain, or forces a young person to cause pain to self by exercise drills, painful posture, or eating noxious substances.[69] Tools for inflicting bodily pain include paddles, straps, clubs, and stun guns, and the use of painful chemicals like mace. Physical punishment was the main enforcement tool in dominator cultures but is now considered abuse in many democracies, even in the home.

Physical violence is not only common among boys, but increasingly frequent among girls.[70] Studies in the United States found that 60 percent of "worst school experiences" reported by students involved peers, but a surprising 40 percent involved adults. These were not limited to verbal put-downs but also include physically intimidating behaviour.[71] At least half of middle school students experience physical harassment or attack by peers. Corporal punishment in schools is permitted in 23 states in the U.S. with three-quarters of a million incidents documented annually, although many more go unreported.

Children and adolescents rely on adults for protection and are very threatened when caregivers become physically abusive or threaten body or sexual boundaries. A student recalled, "One of the teachers – he threw a kid up against the wall and that was scary." Another said, "Surly aides who have nasty rumours spreading about them make me feel unsafe."[72]

Deprivation versus Nurturance

For optimal development, humans need to be free from want and to feel secure that their basic physical needs will be met. They also need safe and predictable physical environments that contribute to a sense of health and well-being. Some coercive interventions seek to frustrate these basic needs.

Children become highly distressed by discipline which disrupts physiological well-being. Examples include withholding food, sleep, exercise, elimination, hygiene, medical care, clothing, and shelter. This interferes with basic physical and security needs.

Physical surroundings can contribute to a sense of well-being or can be highly distressing. Many residential care facilities are cold, barren, graffiti covered, and poorly equipped and maintained. Problems of noise, crowding, temperature, lighting, sanitation, and air quality are common. Surroundings lack normalcy, beauty, and harmony with nature. Some settings are purposely designed to be austere and uncomfortable to avoid "rewarding" youth for problem behaviour or to inflict "pains of imprisonment." Bruno Bettelheim once compared such conditions to those he encountered as a prisoner in a concentration camp. He proposed creating physical environments that would be a sanctuary for troubled children.[73] An environment of beauty is a silent teacher conveying to youth that they are of value. Surroundings of ugliness send equally powerful messages.

Somehow interventions that would qualify as neglect or abuse have long been seen as acceptable for use with delinquents. A widely publicised early behaviour modification program was conducted at the National Training School in Washington, DC. The behavioural control system relied heavily on a "token economy" which began by depriving youth of basic needs. Boys entered this experimental project on "welfare" status. They lived in bleak surroundings and were forced to earn such basics as decent meals, privacy, and a place for possessions. As might be expected, most youth jumped through whatever hoops were required to earn "privileges." The day the project closed, the students rioted and destroyed the facilities.[74]

Children connect to adults who meet their needs and resist those who obstruct their needs. But deprivation damages social bonds. Further, adults have legal obligations to provide for children, and neglecting this responsibility is evidence of maltreatment.

Restraint versus Freedom

Humans and animals are born to be free. They are endowed with brain programs that trigger alarm if deprived of control of their bodies by physical restraint, confinement, or captivity. Try wrapping your arms tightly around a pet and you are likely to get bitten. Because physical restraint is a threat to survival, it is likely to be experienced as punishment, whether such is intended or not. In subtle or severe forms, physical restraint is used to control or punish troubled children and youth.

Physical restraint includes holds applied by adults or peers. Restraint tools include ropes, straps, cuffs, shackles, jackets, and chairs that impair freedom of movement. Chemical restraints employ drugs, injections, aversive substances, like mace, to overpower behaviour. Locked settings limit physical freedom and seclusion rooms impose severe physical isolation and stimulus deprivation. A particularly cruel torture technique is covering a prisoner's head with a bag to trigger disorientation and panic.

Studies of discipline methods with challenging youth show that physical confrontations are sometimes instigated by staff who goad youth until they lose control. Some discredited therapy methods promote primal rage by restraining disturbed children. More commonly, adults whose authority is challenged take a combative stance that provokes confrontation. A girl recalled a family session where the therapist blocked the door with his chair and commanded, "Talk! Tell your mother what happened." She reported she "freaked out" and was dragged off to seclusion.

> **I had never hit anybody, never hurt anybody.**
> **... they were forcing me into this room and**
> **weren't going to let me out until I told people**
> **what I was thinking. I felt like my world was**
> **collapsing. I didn't feel safe anymore. There was**
> **no place to hide, being locked in this room.**[75]

Both young people and adults sometimes get payoffs from physical encounters.[76] These rewards can include power, excitement, a reputation for toughness, and discharging anger to restore calm. Research suggests that adults most likely to get into physical encounters with troubled youth are those who are low on empathy, and who are accustomed to solving problems by force.[77]

It is difficult to separate physical restraint for bona fide safety needs from that provoked by mishandling behavioural incidents. Even though formal reports are kept, these may not reflect actual details of how behaviour escalated. There is a great disparity in the frequency of restraint and seclusion in various settings serving similar populations. Once expectations are established that restraint or seclusion will be used, there is an erosion of boundaries: Young people are primed to get into physical encounters and adults feel behavioural control is dependent upon these extreme interventions. Restraint and seclusion are not limited to dangerous behaviour but are widely used as sanctions for noncompliance and defiance.[78] This is particularly troubling since restraint can cause injury and death. Further, seclusion triggers self-destructive thoughts and increases risk of self-harm or suicide.[79]

Emotional Coercion

Emotional coercion produces psychological distress and interferes with the normal development of emotional resilience.[80] This includes threat, hostility, and blame. In contrast, emotional support involves trust, respect, and understanding.

Threat versus Trust

"As soon as we judge that something is threatening, we feel repelled from it, we feel urged to avoid it."[81] Thus, only those who pass the "trust test" with young persons are able to engage them. This is a positive connection in which parties work cooperatively towards mutually agreed goals.[82] But threat and intimidation create fear and lead to avoidance or adversarial contests. Examples include verbal threats, shouting, swearing, invading space, and menacing looks and gestures. Peers also use bullying and group intimidation.

Threat is sometimes used to establish authority. The display of power enforced by angry emotion presumably warns kids to be wary of this adult. Rachel, a young person who lived on the streets of Sydney, Australia, described her reactions to adults who approached her in a domineering manner:

**They don't listen. They tell you to shut up. They
flaunt their authority. When people try to ram
things down my throat, I want to rebel. I'll do the
complete opposite of what they want. Staff can't
be the dominator. When I can share with staff,
there is an aura of respect.**

Angry, hostile confrontation is even purported to be a
"treatment" method as a therapist or group tries to break down
defences and exercise control. After the sudden death of his father,
fourteen-year-old Allan displayed troubled behaviour in school. He
describes being ripped from his family and shipped to a residential
program where peers were used to punish problem behaviour.

**I hated this place and they hated me. During the
general meeting, the other kids were required to
"confront" the person who had problems. They
would surround you and yell, scream, and swear.
If this didn't work, the group would restrain you
on the floor..., I hated being restrained and kept
fighting them. When restraint wouldn't work, the
next punishment was to place the kid in "The
Ring." Staff put boxing gear on me. The other
kids would surround me, joining arms. Three
bigger, tougher boys took turns fighting me to
teach me a lesson.**[83]

Some so-called "therapy" methods are highly confrontational
and intrusive. A book on family treatment advises parents of
troubled youth to prepare for "atom bomb interventions" including
taking clothes away, forcing youth to dress as nerds, selling their
possessions, and confining them to the bathroom for as many hours
as they have run away.[84] Some group programs place youth on a
"hot seat" to break down defences and force disclosure.

While children need controls on behaviour, *intrusive discipline*
dictates thoughts and feelings.[85] Any disagreement is stifled by
demands of absolute loyalty and obedience to those in power.
Intrusive discipline often is accompanied with the threat of love
withdrawal as if the youth were property owned by another.
Intrusive discipline is emotional abuse and produces serious
problems, including both acting out and internalising behaviours. In
contrast, resilience requires personal power and self-efficacy, so

one can exercise inner control and distance oneself from destructive influences.

While youth need to develop self-discipline, the obedience model requires submission to an all-powerful authority. Demands for absolute obedience easily deteriorate into abuse. Children need trusting relationships with adults and peers who can provide emotional support.

Hostility versus Respect

Children who are treated with love and respect come to believe they are persons of value. But those who feel unwanted and rejected neither respect themselves or others. The most damaging methods of discipline are hostile, demeaning acts that convey dislike and rejection. Such treatment triggers shame and feelings of worthlessness. Some rejected persons turn their shame against others in hate and hostility. Specific behaviours that convey rejection include ridicule, name-calling, scapegoating, shunning, and various verbal and nonverbal signals of indifference, contempt, and exclusion.

Patronising treatment can be wrapped in the guise of "helping" by sending messages that one is inferior or inadequate. More overt rejection is seen in acts of bigotry and hate which demean individuals because of their family, friends, religion, race, culture, class, gender, age, sexual orientation, disability, or appearance. Prejudicial behaviour operates on a continuum of speaking ill of others, discriminating, segregating, attacking, and destroying.[86]

In any setting for young people, adults have a legal and moral obligation to prevent climates of hostility, but such is common. In many schools, popular students like male athletes use their strength to ostracise or demean peers they label as "weird." Homosexual youth are five times as likely as others to miss school because of fear of such hostility, and harassing interactions are common among both girls and boys.[87] Those most at risk for peer hostility include children with disabilities, minority populations, and non-assertive, weaker, or socially different children.

Admittedly, kids who present problems can evoke great frustration for those who live and work with them. Many adults want to avoid or get rid of such young persons. A high school teacher in a training on youth at risk said, "My job is to teach the 70 per cent who are good kids; it's not worth wasting time on the others." A principal in another school bragged that his job was to "amputate" troublesome students.

Many who "demand respect" forget that in its most basic meaning respect requires treating others the way we wish to be treated, which of course is the Golden Rule. Acts that disrespect youth fuel disrespect and defiance.

Blame versus Understanding

Young persons need understanding adults and peers who look beneath their problems to show empathy and concern. To understand is not to excuse behaviour, but to separate the deed from the doer.[88] Blame and fault-finding are simplistic thinking errors that exaggerate flaws, obscure strengths and assume the worst about a person.

Blame is conveyed in overt criticism as well as in nonverbal signals, such as tone of voice and signs of irritation, annoyance, and condemnation. Some in authority believe harsh confrontation is tough love while empathy is weak and ineffectual. But belittling criticism creates a sense of inadequacy that interferes with the ability to creatively solve problems. Human brains process blame as threat and are unlikely to learn from such criticism.

Adults greatly overuse preaching and scolding. Reprimands are the most frequent interventions used by elementary and junior high teachers who deliver one reprimand every two minutes. Some young people just tune out such nattering. Others become more defiant under a barrage of parental and teacher criticism. Research shows that positive teacher support decreases inappropriate student behaviour, but such is rare in many programs for troubled students.[89]

Blame is a universal brain program of emotional logic which primes humans to identify and attack a perceived enemy. Blame is often confused with responsibility which involves owning one's behaviour and being accountable to others. Blame blocks empathy and esteem and prevents one from showing concern for another. A mindset of blame interferes with understanding the perspective of another person and reading the motives behind their actions.

Blame and empathy are incompatible brain states. Blame is driven by personal negative emotions. But in empathy, our brain tunes in to the emotions of another person.[90] While empathy is innate, it cannot develop properly without experience in caring bonds. Persons who lack empathy are self-centred and indifferent to what another person may feel or need. Empathy is a critical building block of resilience.[91]

Social Coercion

Children have universal needs for belonging, mastery, independence, and generosity. Social coercion restricts these normal growth needs through exclusion, frustration, domination, and unconcern.

Exclusion versus Belonging

Needs for attachment are met by supportive relationships in the family, peer group, school, and community. Since children have strong motivations for social contact, restricting this is a potent punishment. This entails withholding contact with friends and peers, even if they are a positive influence. In settings where youth are separated from families, it is a common practice to treat the right to family contact as if it were a privilege dependent on acceptable behaviour.

Suspension and expulsion in schools cut youth off from normal relationships. Other coercive management methods that block socialization include lengthy time out, rules against physical contact, and the silent treatment. Youth may be deprived of normal bonds by being placed in settings where they are forced to be in contact with disliked or feared persons. Ironically many programs that segregate troubled youth are impoverished of social support. A child can go through an entire day without any positive social interactions with another person.[92]

Frustration versus Mastery

Children hate boredom and naturally seek challenging, goal-directed activity. As they explore their interests, they develop creative problem-solving abilities.[93] But frustration results whenever a desired activity or goal is blocked.[94] Thus, restricting normal interests and activities can be a painful punishment. Examples are withholding participation in recreation or learning activities, such as athletics, trips, cultural ceremonies, religious involvement, school activities, and even school attendance. Management by "overcorrection" tries to modify behaviour by tedious repetition of an action. In reality, this is punishment by imposing meaningless, frustrating work.

Obstructing involvement in desired activities has short-term punitive power, but interferes with long-term learning. Young persons need a rich menu of activities even if their behaviour does not suggest they "deserve" this.[95]

Of course, restricting participation in activities a child is not able to handle is a natural consequence. Likewise, research supports sequencing activities whereby less desirable tasks are completed before enjoyable activities. This Premack Principle is sometimes called "Grandma's rule". Children are better able to manage natural, logical consequences than contrived consequences intended to cause frustration.

Many so-called *token economies* withhold desired activities or resources. In contrast to positive reinforcement, such frustration leads to aggression or withdrawal. We see many examples of children in pain who keep digging themselves into a hole by losing so many points they abandon any hope of positive experiences. Some years ago, Texas passed a law to restrict participation in sports if students had low grades. In spite of public popularity, research showed that being removed from a school athletic team increased gang involvement instead of grades.[96]

Domination versus Independence

Young people need opportunities to learn to make decisions and to exercise personal power.[97] As African-American educator W. E.B. Dubois once said, responsibility is the first step in responsibility. But obedience-training models of discipline create powerlessness instead of self-control.

The development of autonomy and independence is retarded by rigid rules and adult-imposed routines. Schools and youth programs are often built around long lists of regulations and penalties. "But they have to learn to follow rules in life" is the common rationale of those in power. That might make sense if the rules imposed matched those in the real world. Many simply limit a young person's freedom without teaching any core values. Recurrent examples are contests about style of dress or grooming. Even when a rule is sensible, it may be carried out in foolish ways that fail to respect the young person's need to learn from failure. One wealthy school district proposed fining any student who was late for class one hundred dollars. Presumably this rule will not apply to teachers.

When punishments don't stop rule breaking, more are administered. If doctors worked this way, they would double dosages of medications that create ill effects. Research on effective alternative schools challenges the myth that "clear rules and consequences" are effective with disruptive students. Successful schools modify rules to respond to the needs of non-adjusting students.[98] This does not mean that permissiveness will work since children need structure and order. Effective mentors are those who can hold youth accountable as well as respond to their needs.[99]

In an overreaction to fears of school violence, levels of security exceed supervision needs and undercut the capacity of youth for self-governance. Invasive monitoring and surveillance limits privacy. Arbitrary reward and punishment systems seek to impose order. But rules not embraced by the governed will be flouted. A saying common among early youth work pioneers was that building walls only makes wall-climbing a sport.

Unconcern versus Generosity

Positive values develop in a climate of mutual concern where individuals treat others as persons of value. Living in mutual concern with significant others gives life meaning and purpose. But without the opportunity to give and receive kindness, young people remain self-centred and lack empathy.

While love was a central concept in early educational philosophy, close bonds between adults and youth are frowned on in depersonalised schools and authoritarian institutions. Yet, resilience research shows that "simple sustained kindness – a touch on the shoulder, a smile, a greeting – have powerful corrective impact."[100]

Presumably to avoid "pampering" young persons, kindness is simply not allowed in some settings. When adult-youth contacts are severely limited to formal social roles, any strong attachments between a youth and adult are likely to be seen as suspect. In environments where kindness and love are in short supply, caring for others is not fashionable. This is seen in hostile peer cultures marked by ridicule, harassment, racism, and exclusion of any who are "different." Adult-youth encounters are also adversarial or aloof. Ultimately, unless values of concern are modelled and taught by adults, one cannot create caring cultures.

Behavioural researchers found that in positive programs, youth and adults frequently interact in proximity of less than three feet of distance.[101] But in many settings, the norms forbid expressions of warmth. Conversations of child and youth care workers on an international website decry regulations that build gulfs between caregivers and children. One worker reported his setting even required staff to ask permission to give a "high five" handshake to a youth. Professionals from Germany toured a residential program for young women in the U.S. They questioned why there was a rule that neither staff nor residents were allowed any physical contact. "We think hugging is therapy," said the puzzled visitors.

Nick Long contends that the most powerful therapeutic method is kindness.[102] The root of the word "kindness" is "kin" and refers to treating others as if they were related.[103] Generosity calls for giving and forgiving even if the natural reaction to difficult behaviour is to strike back in anger. The most dangerous persons are those deprived of kindness and love. Those who are unable to receive and reciprocate kindness live self-centred and purposeless lives.

In sum, a wide variety of coercive strategies are used with problem behaviour, although there is little likelihood these can remedy pain-based behaviour. Applying negative consequences might provide short-term compliance but does nothing to build controls from within.

The Powerlessness of Punishment

Intimidation is an acknowledgement of the weakness of your point of view.
— Desmond Tutu[104]

The effectiveness of "get tough" approaches is greatly exaggerated. A colleague[105] described how the Irish Republican Army [IRA] tried in vain to control youthful car thieves, called "joy riders," with the most severe punishments imaginable. The IRA would drive these boys from the community, but they returned. Families would be threatened. When all else failed, youth would be taken out and "knee-capped" with a bullet fired through each leg to cripple them. But as soon as the joy riders could hobble out of the hospital with casts and crutches, they would defiantly steal another car. Punishment only fuelled "angry pride" and hardened hatred of punishers.

Punishment motivates rebellion rather than teaching responsible self-control.[106] Young people with histories of abuse by adults construe coercive discipline as hostile attacks.[107] Punishment reinforces the bias that the world is hostile and respect must be gained by threat and coercion.[108]

Coercive discipline can complicate racial distrust. Leon Fulcher of New Zealand suggests that such treatment can threaten "cultural safety" when dealing with youth who come from backgrounds, such as Maori, where discipline is based on respect.[109] Those who lack understanding of youth from other cultures are also more likely to be threatened by challenging behaviour and respond in ways that cause racial conflict.[110]

Coercive discipline triggers powerful stress reactions sparking fear and frustration.[111] Hostile criticism stirs angry feelings. Restraint and isolation are highly destructive to mental health. The immediate brain effects of coercive conflicts can endure for many hours, keeping the individual on edge and hyper-reactive to provocation. Recurrent coercive treatment can cause permanent changes in personality as persons develop reactive patterns of defensiveness or hostility.

Coercive discipline models bullying. Studies in natural camp settings showed that children subjected to autocratic adult leaders reproduce this pattern among their own peers. When not directly supervised by authority, the youngsters expressed hostility for their adult leaders and bullied and scapegoated weaker youngsters.[112]

Decades of research show that coercion propels youngsters on the pathway to problem behaviour. When a child is in distress, the responsive adult acts to meet the child's needs and calms the child.[113] But if caregivers react with hostility – or if they indulge tantrums – the dance of disturbance begins. Participants in coercive cycles display negative behaviour, emotions, and thinking towards one another.[114]

Coercive discipline contaminates the relationship between a troubled young person and those who could provide positive guidance. Social control comes from positive social bonds to family, elders, school staff, mentors, and positive peers.[115] These relationships are protective factors that prevent high risk behaviour.

Punishment packs a punch by causing physical, social, or emotional pain. Paradoxically, problem behaviour springs from physical, emotional, or social pain. While the threat of punishment may compel compliance, it does little to build the strengths of youth.

A New Pathway

For a century, debate about problem behaviour has swirled around punishment versus rehabilitation. Punishment uses coercion to control deviance. Rehabilitation focuses on treating disorder. Thus, punishment and rehabilitation are not really opposites since both involve pessimistic, fault-finding mindsets.[116] In contrast, restorative methods are grounded in respectful values and the science of positive youth development. Restorative practices are not new; this was the "natural" process of discipline practiced for centuries in societies that deeply valued their young.

Coercive and restorative strategies each seek positive behaviour but are opposite in their thrust. Coercion blocks the very needs that are essential for positive growth:

- *Physical Coercion* produces physiological distress.
- *Physical Support* fosters physiological well-being.

- *Emotional Coercion* produces psychological distress.
- *Emotional Support* fosters psychological well-being.

- *Social Coercion* frustrates normal growth needs.
- *Social Support* fosters positive growth and development.

Pioneering child psychiatrist Richard Jenkins cautioned that we may not always have available enough positive methods and relationships to deal with highly challenging children without some use of coercion.[117] However, unless positives predominate, management efforts are likely to be futile.[118]

Children need both love and limits to thrive. However, coercion relies on punishment and adult-dominated controls to force obedience. Restorative approaches build strengths that enable youth to overcome problems and change the course of their life pathways.

3

The Resilience Revolution

> *Given sufficient support humans can defy the odds and become agents of history.*
> — Dr. Mamphela Ramphele[119]

The Spirit of Optimism

For hundreds of years, some leading thinkers challenged the view that children were basically evil. Dutch educator and clergyman Erasmus (1466-1536) saw harsh punishment as adults indulging their passions rather than correcting the errors of children. In France, Montaigne (1533-1592) proclaimed "Away with violence!" and called for eliminating discipline by "horror and cruelty."[120] After the Napoleonic Wars, Pestalozzi (1746-1827) founded orphanages for street children. He took the scriptural call to "become as a little child" to mean that adults should treat children with deep respect, as equals before the creator. But these were clearly minority views in cultures where power was the measure of one's worth.

The rise of democracy posed the first serious challenge to coercive practices. In nation after nation, youth work pioneers proclaimed that positive potentials existed in the most devalued children and teens.[121] Rabindrinath Tagore established schools for cast-off children in India, describing them in stirring poetry that brought him the Nobel Prize in literature. Anton Makarenko gathered together street children who terrorised Soviet cities after the Russian Revolution and created schools to teach them "joy."

Maria Montessori took on the challenge of educating children from Rome's slums to prove that they had absorbent minds.

None was a greater champion of children than Janusz Korczak who established schools for the street children of Warsaw.[122] He noted that prejudice toward the young persisted long after other forms of discrimination and slavery had been abandoned. Korczak called for treating each child not as a *future citizen* but rather as a *citizen in embryo*. He challenged both capitalist and communist systems for treating children as economic commodities rather than persons with dignity:

The market value of the very young is small. Only in the sight of God and the Law is the apple blossom worth as much as the apple, green shoots as much as a field of ripe corn.[123]

Dorothea Dix (1802-1887) became aware of the mistreatment of youth when she taught Sunday school to incarcerated girls. She crusaded in North America, Europe, and Asia for enlightened "moral treatment" based on compassion and respect. This mental health movement was sparked by idealistic young physicians who worked on the front lines in small mental hospitals to create close relationships with their patients.[124] Restraint and locked isolation were virtually eliminated, and most residents were able to heal and return to their communities.[125]

In 1900, Ellen Key of Sweden wrote of "soul murder in the schools" and called for an end to hostile and demeaning punishment. Corporal punishment was being questioned as the centrepiece of school discipline; frankly it just didn't work in a free society. A typical Boston public school of the era housed 400 pupils and gave 65 whippings a day, one every six minutes, almost an assembly line. In hundreds of rural schools, students were driving punitive teachers away.[126]

The modern juvenile court was founded in Chicago in 1899 by social worker Jane Addams. Children were removed from adult prisons to be provided care appropriate to their needs. The children's court soon spread to all democratic nations. These philosophies led to many schools for wayward youth based on self-governance. In Berlin, Karl Wilker transformed the most abusive institution by replacing bars and barbed wire with positive bonds between adults and youth. In an important book on youth empowerment, Wilker wrote:

What we want to achieve in our work with young people is to find and strengthen the positive and healthy elements, no matter how deeply they are hidden. We enthusiastically believe in the existence of those elements even in the seemingly worst of our adolescents. [127]

With the rise of Hitler, Wilker's books were burned and he fled to South Africa where he resumed teaching disadvantaged students. There another educator and author, Alan Paton, would replicate reforms in the Diepkloof reformatory for Black children.[128] He decried a society that punishes and destroys the very youth it corrupts. Rejecting racist and dehumanising methods, Paton built relationships, responsibility, and respect. His program became known world-wide as a model of enlightened practice.

In spite of the contributions of these reformers, progressive ideas were slow to take hold. Democracy was a fragile flower and harsh discipline was still in style. There were no training programs to prepare new generations of professionals in positive methods. Further, there was not yet a solid science of positive youth development.

By mid-twentieth century the hopefulness of earlier decades had given way to pessimistic views.[129] Troubled kids were described as disruptive, disobedient, disturbed, and disordered. Such labels masked their needs and potential greatness.

Still, influential persons called for a return to a positive psychology. Carl Rogers showed that children could overcome very difficult backgrounds by gaining insight into their circum- stances and taking responsibility for their behaviour.[130] Anna Freud studied a group of orphaned children rescued from Nazi concentration camps.[131] While totally antagonistic to all adults, the children showed amazing loyalty, love, and self-sacrifice to one another. Fritz Redl reported research on the problems of aggre- ssive children, but suggested another book could be written on their unrecognised virtues.[132] Australian therapist Michael White rejected the deficit view most succinctly: "Pathology. The word makes me wince."[133]

The most eminent psychiatrist in the twentieth century was Karl Menninger (1893-1990) who blasted his profession for its pessimistic views on the human condition. When in his nineties, Dr. Karl was asked which of his many books would have the most enduring impact, he quickly chose The Vital Balance which he had written in 1963.[134] That work described three stages in the history of mental health:

- Yesterday marked the discovery of mental illness.
- Today we focus on methods for prevention and treatment.
- Tomorrow we will discover how persons can become *weller than well*.

Dr. Menninger accurately foretold a science of resilience where even life's disruptions could strengthen human character. His prototype of "weller than well" was William James who overcame serious personal problems to achieve eminence in both psychology and philosophy. A century ago, James wrote: "The potentialities of development in human souls are unfathomable."[135]

The American Psychological Association is now calling for research on strengths like courage, responsibility, and hope: "Much of the task of prevention in this new century will be to understand and learn how to foster these virtues in young people."[136] In this spirit, Zvi Levy of Israel offers youth this message: "What is in you is good enough to take you to places you have never dared to go."[137]

From Deficits to Strengths

Glance at problems, gaze at strengths.
— J. C. Chambers

Resilience science is a relatively recent arrival on the psychological scene. A leading researcher described resilience as achieving positive life outcomes in spite of risk.[138] Resilience also involves the ability to rebound from adversity with greater strength to meet future challenges.[139] Research shows that even serious disruptions in a child's life can offer unexpected opportunities for growth.[140]

Initially, some believed that resilience was a rare trait of a few "invulnerable" super-kids. But studies following high risk children into adulthood found that 60 percent eventually made positive adjustments.[141] Even children exposed to severe trauma can turn their lives around if they can find supportive persons.[142] Far from being a rare quality, humans are by nature resilient, for we are all descendants of survivors. The other side of the coin is that there are no invulnerable persons, for if our basic needs are frustrated, we all are at risk.

We are now in the midst of a resilience revolution sparked by exciting research on children who successfully surmount terrible backgrounds. Prominent resilience researchers include Emmy Werner and Ruth Smith who followed high-risk Hawaiian children into adulthood; most turned out well in spite of a rocky early history.[143] Similar studies were conducted by Michael Rutter of England on the Isle of Wight.[144] Others have studied resilience in special populations as varied as delinquents, survivors of war, and street children. According to a prominent researcher, "if there is any lesson to be derived from recent studies, it lies in the reaffirmation of the resilience potential that exists in children under stress."[145] Of course resilience not only involves inner strength in the young person, but support from those in the environment.

The view that is emerging is that humans are by nature potentially resilient. We have inherited from our ancestors a resilient brain that possesses bioprograms for survival and well-being. *Strengths* are positive personal qualities or virtues. *Growth needs* are brain-based motivational programs that help foster social harmony and personal competence. When growth needs are met, children develop their strengths. In Circle of Courage terms, these include belonging, mastery, independence, and generosity.

Resilience research broadens our view of problem behaviour beyond narrow psychiatric labels.[146] Certainly progress continues to be made in studying brain-based disorders.[147] But prominent child psychiatrists note that only a few disorders, such as autism, appear to fit the classical medical model. Many of the most common childhood problems – like anger, fear, impulsiveness, inattention, and moodiness – are part of normal development or result from stressful environments.[148] Such problems are best addressed by nurturing children's needs and building their strengths.[149]

Communities are not equally effective in meeting the growth needs of children. Even in wealthy nations, the interests of children can be subservient to other priorities. In the United States, the discrepancy between what children need and receive has led to calls for a national initiative to rebuild the youth development infrastructure.[150]

A developmental, strength-based approach to young people at risk is now at the heart of new policy in South Africa following the work of the Inter-ministerial Committee on Young People at Risk established in 1996 by President Nelson Mandela to transform the

41

child and youth care system. Assessment and intervention in South Africa now focus on the Circle of Courage dimensions of belonging, mastery, independence, and generosity. This philosophy is grounded both in science and in spiritual values as expressed by Archbishop Desmond Tutu:

> **We must look on children in need not as problems but as individuals with potential to share if they are given the opportunity. Even when they are really troublesome, there is some good in them, for, after all, they were created by God. I would hope we could find creative ways to draw out of our children the good that is there in each of them.**[151]

The Resilient Human Brain

There is rich evidence that the human mind is designed to "solve" the important problems all persons face for survival and well-being.[152] For example, we build bonds to others in order to learn from them and protect ourselves against danger. This is not coincidence since the brain is formatted with *universal logic* or "decision rules" that motivate behaviour. Therefore, a person in crisis is automatically programmed to seek support from a trusted companion.

For each of the universal problems humans have faced throughout their history, there are specific brain programs that provide a logical course of action. These are activated by stimuli or information that signals we face a certain problem or challenge. Once this universal logic is triggered by the brain, we are strongly motivated, often unconsciously, to follow a particular course of action.

Resilience requires abilities to survive and thrive, even in the face of difficulty. All humans are by nature resilient, having inherited these capacities from ancestors who overcame all manner of hardship. Although specific methods of coping may vary with individuals and culture, resilience is universal because it is based on the innate capacity of the human brain.[153]

How can we make sense of the mushrooming literature on the science of resilience and positive youth development? The Circle of Courage has been described as *The Resilience Code* because it translates strength-building research into a concise and understandable format.[154] The Resilience Code is more than a metaphor; it describes universal human growth needs. The key landmarks on the journey to resilient outcomes are Belonging, Mastery, Independence, and Generosity.

The Circle of Courage

Belonging is developed through opportunities to build trusting bonds of human attachment.

Mastery requires opportunities to creatively solve problems and meet goals for achievement.

Independence *is fostered* by opportunities to grow in responsibility and autonomy.

Generosity is shown through opportunities to show concern in acts of kindness and altruism.

Research on Self-Worth

Significance
"I am important to someone."

Competence
"I am able to solve problems."

Power
"I am in charge of my life."

Virtue
"I am considerate to others."

There is a close connection between the Circle of Courage and other research on strengths and resilience. The classic early study of strengths in children is *The Antecedents of Self Esteem* by Stanley Coopersmith.[155] He found that children build their sense of self-worth on the foundations of significance, competence, power, and virtue. As shown in the accompanying table, these parallel the four dimensions of the Circle of Courage. More recently, a review of common themes of various studies of resilience identifies the needs that children have for affiliation, competence, autonomy, and purpose.[156]

Resilience develops naturally as children are able to meet growth needs. We thought it would also be illustrative to take the findings of three important studies of resilience and overlay these on the Circle of Courage concepts. As shown in the accompanying table, The Resilience Code, there is a high level of agreement. Resilience studies provide rich details of strengths. The Circle of Courage explains how these strengths develop.

From Risk to Resilience

The word *risk* is a synonym for danger. When terms like *children at risk* first came into use, this referred to *dangers in the environment,* like poverty or abuse. But over time, this evolved into a subtle shift to presumed deficits in *at risk youth*. Some current risk assessment approaches mirror this shift by profiling those thought to pose a danger because of their problem behaviour. The resilience revolution turns this thinking around, seeing all children at risk as potential children of promise.

Children whose physical and emotional needs are met show little high-risk behaviour.[157] But when these basic needs are blocked, all manner of difficulties follow. Perhaps the most extensive research on risk and resilience comes from studies of Developmental Assets by the Search Institute.[158] This is a list of forty assets which lead to positive outcomes in youth development. Twenty are *internal assets* like responsibility, achievement motivation, and interpersonal competence. Twenty are *external assets* like family support, positive peer influence, and a caring school climate. Internal assets are *strengths* within the young person; external assets are *supports* provided by families, mentors, schools, and communities.

Studies in hundreds of communities show that youth with many developmental assets usually turn out well. Those with few assets are at risk for a host of bad outcomes, including substance abuse, reckless sexuality, school failure, emotional problems, and delinquency. Remarkably, in a typical community 60 percent of youth have fewer than 20 assets. Youth with ten or fewer of these assets show an average of nine high-risk behaviours. In contrast, kids with more than 30 assets average only one risky behaviour. It couldn't be simpler: *positive growth comes from meeting growth needs.*

A theme running through all studies of resilience is the importance of meeting universal growth needs. We now have a formidable body of research on the crucial needs for attachment, achievement, autonomy, and altruism. These findings are briefly highlighted overleaf from the perspective of the Circle of Courage.

THE RESILIENCE CODE

Belonging: *Developing Attachment.*
- A network of friends, a community where one is respected, humour. (Flach)
- Caring and attentive family environments; if parents are absent or inattentive, extended family, siblings, and other adults provide counsel, safety, and support; participation in school and community programs. (Werner & Smith)
- Relationships, humour, intimate and fulfilling ties to others. (Wolin & Wolin)

Mastery: *Developing Achievement.*
- Creativity, open-mindedness, receptive to new ideas, wide range of interests, recognises ones gifts and talents, willing to dream, finds novel solutions to meet goals, redefines assumptions and problems to find solutions. (Flach)
- High expectations, academic success, communication skills. (Werner & Smith)
- Insight, initiative, creativity, takes on demanding tasks, asks tough questions, gives honest answers, brings order and purpose to chaos. (Wolin & Wolin)

Independence: *Developing Autonomy.*
- Autonomy, independence of thought and action, personal discipline and responsibility, insight into one's own feelings, high tolerance of distress, distances oneself from destructive relationships. (Flach)
- Personal efficacy, control over one's environment. (Werner & Smith)
- Independence, keeps boundaries and emotional distance from troubled persons, initiative, takes charge of problems, exerts control. (Wolin & Wolin)

Generosity: *Developing Altruism.*
- Insight into the feelings of others, hope, commitment, the search for meaning, purpose, faith, a sense of destiny. (Flach)
- Empathy, caring, productive roles in family and community. (Werner & Smith)
- Relationships of empathy, capacity to give, morality with an informed conscience, judges right from wrong, values decency, compassion, honesty, fair play, responds to needs and suffering of others. (Wolin & Wolin)

Sources of Resilience Research

Frederic Flach. (1989). *Resilience: Discovering a New Strength at Times of Stress.* New York: Fawcett Columbine.
Emmy Werner & Ruth Smith. (1992). *Overcoming the Odds: High Risk Children from Birth to Adulthood.* Ithaca, NY: Cornell University Press.
Steven Wolin & Sybil Wolin. (1993). *The Resilient Self.* New York: Villard.

Belonging: Developing Attachment

An array of evidence shows that humans possess a fundamental need to belong.[159] This is fulfilled by frequent positive interactions with at least a few persons who share mutual concern. Belonging creates positive emotions, particularly pride; rejection produces shame, among the most painful social emotions humans can experience.

The desire to form attachments is encoded in the human DNA. For example, the human brain has an area for reading emotions on the face which is different from perception of inanimate objects. Attachment behaviour has been studied across the life span from infancy through the expanding relationships of childhood, adolescence, and adulthood.[160]

Recent brain research shows that smiling and laughter are powerful social bonding mechanisms.[161] Simply, friends are fun. In any cluster of kids, smiles and peals of laughter permeate interactions. Laughter and smiling are signs of belonging.[162] Humour lowers barriers and fosters trust as we exchange instinctual bonding signals. One attraction of alcohol is that it primes the laugh mechanism of the brain. Laughter has long been seen as therapeutic as noted in the Proverbs: "A merry heart doeth good like a medicine."[163] Laughter has a darker side when used to exclude outsiders, such as with social ridicule.

Contrary to early speculation that humans were inherently aggressive animals, it is now clear that we are innately friendly beings who are inclined to form strong, enduring, and harmonious attachments with others of the species – or as Harlow simply put it, to love them.[164] It is no accident that love is the most frequently cited word in *Bartlett's Book of Quotations*.

Mastery: Developing Achievement

A central motivation behind much human behaviour is the quest to become competent.[165] Children can acquire a mass of knowledge, including an entire language code, without formal instruction. The human brain creates order out of chaos and solves the problems necessary for social and personal survival. The talents of young persons can only crystallise with the support of adult mentors or more skilful peers.[166]

The brain operates best with tasks that are challenging but not boring or overwhelming. This is called JMD which is shorthand for

Just Manageable Difficulty.[167] By mastering new skills, children are better equipped to face future challenges. "Task motivation" from the joy of accomplishment is preferable to "egoistic motivation" where individuals are mainly concerned with how they compare to others.

Problem solving has been studied for a century since John Dewey first suggested that all goal-directed behaviour begins with some "felt difficulty."[168] Practical intelligence is the ability to creatively solve problems and meet one's goals by capitalising on strengths and overcoming weaknesses.[169] Successfully intelligent people defy negative expectations, such as low scores on tests. They do not let others stop them from achieving their goals. They find their path and pursue it, realising that there will be obstacles along the way and that surmounting these is part of the challenge. Successfully intelligent youth seek out role models. They also observe people who fail and make sure they do things differently.

In Western culture, intelligence is viewed as a narrow set of academic skills measured by tests. Other societies place high emphasis upon skills fostering interpersonal harmony. In Zambia, intelligent children are socially responsible, cooperative, and respectful. In Zimbabwe, the word for intelligence is *ngware* which means to be skilled in social relationships. In Kenya, intelligent children are those who are responsible, verbally quick, and successfully manage interpersonal relationships. Likewise, parents of Latino and Asian youth may highly prize social competence.[170]

Research on intelligence has progressed beyond narrow verbal and computational skills to include practical, social, and emotional intelligence.[171] There is little connection between intelligence and raising test scores. Turning schools into test-prep centres actually stifles learning, says our colleague Linda Lantieri. There is an old saying that *You can't fatten a goat by weighing it*. "Letting children know how dumb they are won't make them smart."[172] Instead, children need opportunities to develop problem-solving ability, talent, and creativity.

Independence: Developing Autonomy

All young persons desire to control their lives and influence events in their social world.[173] Some act as pilots, setting the course toward personal goals. Others are more like robots who react automatically to events which surround them.[174] Psychologists use the terms *internal locus of control* and *external locus of control* to describe persons who feel in charge of their lives and those who feel they are pawns of others.[175]

Resilient youth develop personal autonomy. Even if life is difficult, they have confidence they can make things better. They are able to stand up to negative influence and are not easily misled by others. They distance themselves emotionally from friends or troubled family members, setting their own pathway.[176]

It may seem contradictory, but close attachments to caregivers actually foster independence. Those who learn to trust others are better able to trust themselves. Still, some youth who have not benefited from close adult guidance can actually become very self-reliant because they have had to learn to depend on themselves.

Before about eight years of age, most children think adults are in charge of the world. Thereafter, they quickly discover that adults are not all-powerful.[177] The biggest developmental change as children move into adolescence is a heightened desire for autonomy. This can create conflicts with adults who still expect children to act submissive.

Many behaviours that irritate adults are landmarks on the road to independence. Children test their strength with loudness and physical horseplay. Teens show bravado and risk-taking and push the limits of adult control. Rule-breaking becomes a practice run at independence. In the ensuing power struggles, youth seek autonomy while adults seek to control. Youth need pro-social outlets for their growing need for independence.

Generosity: Developing Altruism

Humans function best when they are part of a community of mutual social support. As they fulfil obligations to others, they discover that they are valued and esteemed.[178] But for decades, psychology operated as if all human behaviour were selfishly motivated. Now, research on altruism has shown that caring for others is central to human nature.[179] Moral development studies show what the great religious traditions long have taught, that concern for others is the foundation of character and morality.[180] Children learn morality by how they are treated rather than what they are told.[181]

Kurt Hahn, founder of Outward Bound, noted that many modern youth suffer from the "misery of unimportance" and long to be used in some demanding cause. An "I'll-get-mine" culture leaves students self-absorbed and devoid of purpose. Generosity is an antidote for this narcissism. Giving to others develops higher levels of moral development and provides youth a sense of purpose. Those who were once societal liabilities become valuable assets.

Through helping others, young persons discover they have the power to influence their world in a positive manner. Those who themselves come from troubled backgrounds are often the most responsive to others in need. Such was the case with a boy named Lance who noted:

> **I feel that the greatest thing one could give to another student is friendship. People who come from a negative home life, school is all they can look forward to and count on. I try to be nice to people and talk to people no one else will. I try to make them feel good about themselves. I do it a lot.**[182]

Genuine helping requires a spirit of generosity which reaches out in empathy to another. The philosopher Martin Buber concluded that those who set out to help others to satisfy their own needs are using others as objects.[183] An authentic relationship is grounded in a deep respect.

Children ask the same questions as adults as they seek to find meaning in life.[184] Youth whose lives are in pain and turmoil are among those most likely to pose deeply spiritual questions like "Why was I even born?" and "What is the reason to go on living?" Perhaps the best way young persons can find meaning in life is to commit to a purpose beyond self.[185] We once asked teens in a detention centre if they had any hopes or dreams for their future. One boy responded, "No. That's why we're here." As young people gain an understanding of their worth and value, they discover a sense of calling for their life.

In the foreword to the book, *No Disposable Kids*, Muhammad Ali observes that there are many young persons without hope, but none are hopeless. He summarises the challenge of developing courage and resilience:

> **Kids in conflict are trying to live the best they can with the hand they've been dealt. It is not always easy, since life is not equally kind to us all. We must remember to treat everyone with respect and equality. With new opportunities, many of these youth can rebuild their lives.**[186]

4

Connecting for Support

Our unique relationship is an archetype of possible future relationships.
— Brian Gannon[187]

Disconnected Kids

All children need at least one other person who is irrationally crazy about them, says Urie Bronfenbrenner.[188] But many troubled children have few positive bonds with caring adults. Reaching kids in pain takes special skill. Youngsters who have been hurt before import anger from earlier relationships and target even well-meaning persons who try to help them. Writing of "the student from Hell," Parker Palmer says that it is fear of such youth that shuts down our natural capacity for connection.[189]

A research study on adolescent health interviewed 180,000 teens in order to determine what factors predict staying out of trouble. Emotionally healthy kids answered yes to these two questions: "Do you feel connected at home?" "Do you feel connected at school?" Psychiatrist Robert Hallowell contends that most problems of childhood and youth represent the "diagnosis of disconnection."[190]

Educational pioneers saw positive relationships as the foundation of teaching. In one of the first books written for teachers, Stanley Hall wrote, "If you succeed in gaining their love, your influence will be greater in some respects than that of parents themselves. It will be in your power to direct them into almost any path you choose."[191] In 1925, August Aichhorn of Austria declared that love was the secret to successful work with "wayward youth." Then as now there were those who mocked his view, calling delinquents "the scum of human society, the rabble that populates the prison a few years later."[192] But

Aichhorn saw no scum, only kids in pain. All had received too little genuine love, be it a lack of kindness or an excess of indulgence. In either case, the reaction was the same, hatred and negative behaviour. With this needs assessment, he set out to build a community of mutual respect.

Aichhorn would be shocked at contemporary discussions about "keeping professional distance" from clients. Dr. John Seita, a former troubled youth, is now a resilience expert who contends that the preoccupation with maintaining "boundaries" is often little more than a rationalization for detachment from young persons.[193] Examples of the keep-your-distance mentality abound:

- *Treat them all the same. Don't play favourites.*
- *Don't let children become dependent on you.*
- *Those who get emotionally involved burn out.*
- *Relationships risk accusations of sexual abuse.*
- *Discipline requires keeping your social distance.*

Seita says that relationships change people, not programs. Programs are only of value if they strengthen human connections. Seita's own case file was filled with diagnoses by professionals who were unable to build trust with him. With a touch of humour, he turns the tables and suggests that those who cannot connect with challenging youth can be diagnosed as suffering from *Pessimism Antagonism Detachment Disorder or PADD* for short. The symptoms are these: They assume the worst about youth, and then become involved in antagonistic encounters or detach from interactions.

One symptom of the distance between people in depersonalised Western society is that human touch has been tabooed, says Ashley Montague. It is remarkable that we ignore the input from the largest sense organ of the body, the human skin. We have created a culture of untouchables, strangers to one another who ward off all forms of unnecessary closeness.[194] While some children in pain may not respond well to physical touch, the message from relationship science is clear. All young people need to be touched by some acts of kindness that convey they are valued by others.

Everyday life events provide powerful teaching moments for developing resilience. But those who spend the most time with children seldom have had specific training in how to connect with youth in conflict and help them cope with problems. Such skills are needed by parents, foster parents, educators, child and youth care workers, social workers, psychologists, probation officers, community and faith-based mentors, police, and, of course, peer helpers. In Western Europe and Canada, a front-line child and youth professional is often a highly trained *educateur,* skilled in connecting with reluctant youth.[198] In most other countries, training is very limited and workers do the best they can, using intuitive methods. But a growing knowledge base suggests new ways to connect with adult-wary kids.

Making Connections

There is plenty of rhetoric about the importance of relationships, but this can be a vague concept. In common usage, relationships refer to intimate bonds with relatives, friends, and sexual partners, but not to treatment interventions. A general perception is that building relationships is a slow, intense process. Since busy professionals such as teachers serve large numbers of students, they would seem to have little time for "relationship building" with individuals. Simply, it is seldom possible to invest huge amounts of time in individual children as one might with one's offspring.

Even if one does not have the opportunity to build long-term relationships with numerous children, brief encounters can provide powerful teaching moments for developing meaningful connections.[196] *"Connections" are positive emotional bonds.* Humans are highly social beings who scan our interpersonal world in search of connections with those we encounter.[197] But some children have learned that adults are dangerous, so building connections with them does not come easy. Fortunately, we now know a great deal about how to reach these attachment-wary kids.

Connections depend on the emotional brain more than the logical brain. Two thirds of the meaning in social interaction comes from nonverbal emotional cues like facial expressions, tone of voice, and gestures.[198] Emotional messages are instant and powerful; even first impressions can lead to a quick connection or a hasty retreat. Words do not have very much impact on connection except when used to send positive emotional messages like *"Wow you are great!"* or negative emotional messages like *"You are such a jerk!"*

Connections involve rhythm and harmony.[199] Like a rap song, connections follow a tempo and tune.[200] Recall an awkward encounter where you were out of sync with another person. Persons can be skilful with words but tone deaf to emotional cues. We recall young persons in residential programs who initially could not connect with professional counsellors but quickly warmed up to cooks. Therapy using "techniques" can interfere with the natural process of building connections. Research is clear: *Positive connections require mutual Trust, Respect, and Understanding.* Like the acronym, TRU, these cannot be faked.[201]

Trust

The word trust comes from the German word *trost*, meaning comfort. We seek out people with whom we feel comfortable. We avoid persons who make us feel uncomfortable. This is a two-way street: if certain kids make us uncomfortable, we cause them discomfort as well. When trust is built, we open up and become vulnerable, believing that this person intends no harm. If persons pose either physical or emotional threat, conditions for genuine trust do not exist. While children may submit in obedience to an oppressor, this is learned helplessness rather than trust.[202] Developmental psychologists see trusting bonds as the foundation for all positive growth.[203]

Respect

We gravitate to those who show positive regard and make us feel valued. We pull away to those who feel devalued or detested. Signs of respect, interest, friendliness, and optimism invite youth to approach and engage. A hostile glance or tone of voice warns us to keep our distance. Kids respond best to persons who recognise their strengths and worth. They avoid like a plague those who treat them with disrespect.

Understanding

We connect with persons who respond with empathy to our needs. Empathy involves tuning in to another's emotions. Humans and higher animals have innate ability to "feel" the emotions of others, for example, by reacting with distress to the cry of another mammal. While animals can sense another creature is in pain, they lack logical brains to make sense out of this pain. If empathy is to be more than distress, we must use our higher brain to take the perspective of the other person in order to intelligently respond to their needs. If we cannot understand or predict the behaviour of another, we become uncomfortable or fearful.[204] People who connect can understand each other, often without the exchange of words.

Children who have learned to distrust others are wary of attempts to build connections. Distrust can be amplified by differences of race, gender, and social status. Martin Brokenleg describes how the "historic distrust" of racism can taint initial attempts to connect across the colour line. The principal of a youth prison in Australia gave this example of one of her teachers:

Most of our residents are aboriginal youth, but our teachers are nearly all white. A new teacher came to me concerned that a student had put his hand on her shoulder. This occurred when he thanked her for helping him with a difficult task. She said he seemed very respectful and this brief touching did not appear to be sexual. However, she wondered what she should do if he did this again. "Whatever you do, don't recoil from him," I advised. "In his culture, this is a sign he wants to connect with you. If you are afraid of these students, you will never reach them."

Building trusting connections is not some fuzzy feel-good notion but is based on hard science. Over millions of years, humans have developed elaborate systems for deciding whether to approach or avoid others. Both fearing and craving social contact, we search for clues about all who enter our world. When meeting a stranger, we try to predict whether the person represents danger or opportunity. The brain's *amygdala* is in charge of security screening and carefully checks out eyes, face, tone of voice, and physical demeanour. In an instant, a tentative decision is made as to whether this is a likely friend or foe. Our higher reasoning brain also gets into the act by calculating risks and benefits of reaching out. In the end, we make a very simple decision – to connect or disengage:

- *Connect:* If a person shows friendly intentions and is "interesting" to us, we are curious and motivated to approach. We exchange eye contact, smiles, respectful greetings, handshakes, conversation, humour, and other friendly "bids" for connection.[205] If the individual responds in kind, we connect.
- *Disengage:* If our bid for connection is greeted with indifference or hostility, the emotional brain registers a potential threat. The result is that we avoid persons who make us feel unwanted or uncomfortable. Based on negative cues in facial expressions, voice tone, or awkward conversation, we conclude, "I just can't connect with that person." This provides sufficient rationale for avoiding this individual.

Social bonds are on the line in all interpersonal encounters.[206] If we do not build and repair connections, bonds are damaged or destroyed. The choice is basic, to connect or disengage.

By school age, most of us are adept at social connections with peers and adults. These bonds help shape our thinking, values, and behaviour. This chapter focuses on a particular kind of powerful connection that is provided by mentors.

The term mentor comes from Greek mythology and refers to a "trusted teacher or counsellor." Mentors help an individual gain more creative problem-solving skills than would be possible by acting alone. As shown by developmental research, mentors include both adults as well as capable peers who provide support and guidance.[207]

Mentors employ the power of trust rather than coercion.[208] Trusting connections involve positive thinking, feelings, and behaviour:

1) Positive thinking – optimism rather than pessimism
2) Positive feelings – respect rather than rancour
3) Positive behaviour – cooperation instead of hostility

With some youth, we begin with a 0 to 3 score for negative thinking, feelings, and behaviour. Removing these obstructions to trust takes a concentrated effort. Otherwise, we can spend months or years in strained or superficial contact without ever making a real connection. Mountains of files document failed interventions with our most "impossible" youth who seem to be hopelessly incorrigible. In fact, these are often "therapy veterans" with successful records at outwitting those who try to change their behaviour.[209]

When youth fight adults, this is evidence that they believe adults are not acting in their best interests.[210] Concern is communicated in moment by moment interactions that either strengthen or rupture bonds. Caregivers must learn to stop their own coercive behaviours if they hope to teach the child new means of coping. The devil is in the detail: coercive tactics include negative verbal or nonverbal messages, angry commands, and increasing hostility or avoidance. In contrast problems must become opportunities to engage youth in the search for positive solutions.

Some youth respond very quickly to bids for connection. Others may take longer to feel secure enough to overcome distrust. This does not usually require a huge investment of time, but rather, short, distributed positive interactions. These give the youth time to "case" the adult and gain the courage to connect. With cautious persons, attempts to "rush to intimacy" will be strongly resisted. By nature, humans are suspicious of strangers who attempt "forced teaming" without going through the normal rituals of getting acquainted.[211] Animals are no different. If you move too rapidly to pet a strange dog, you will get bitten.

We met sixteen-year-old Russell when his grandmother brought him in tow to attend a workshop on alternative schools for youth at risk. She introduced him to us and remarked, "Please talk to him; this boy has caused me more trouble than all my sons put together. He got kicked out of school and was sent to an alternative school, but he hates it. He won't talk to his counsellor from the court either."

Russell initially appeared embarrassed and uncomfortable as the only youth in attendance. In a series of short, informal interactions, we used humour to engage him, making sure not to become pushy and drive him away. During the workshop, he sat with his grandmother in the front row and soon became interested in a discussion of how adults have difficulty connecting with youth. When Russell volunteered examples from his own experiences, he was well received by the professionals in attendance. Here are comments he shared:

> **People who try to talk to me don't set up a comfort zone. They just dive in and probe for information about my problems. They are perfect strangers so why should I give them my life history? I just tell them what they need to know. Adults shouldn't be afraid to be friendly and tell a little about themselves and why they want to help kids.**

> **Some adults set themselves above kids. They lay down the law: "You do what I say when I say it!" or "Don't get up without my permission." They would get better results if they would say, "I'd appreciate it if you would help me figure out what you want to happen with your life." Kids listen to adults who listen to them.**

After initially guarded behaviour in a strange situation, Russell connected with many participants at the workshop. Being surrounded by respectful adults was a new experience and he craved this positive attention.

Connecting in Crisis

People are most susceptible to change in times of crisis. The brain has two very different programs for thinking about solutions to serious problems. The first is to withdraw into solitary contemplation. The second is to reach out to a trusted person for support and guidance. Thus, kids wrestling with conflict are already motivated to solve this problem. Of course, they may be flooded with negative emotions and may have learned not to trust others but rely on themselves. Effective mentors avoid initiating or perpetuating hostile interactions and make themselves a safe island in the storm. Nick Long suggests that, when dealing with an upset person, we must be a thermostat to turn down the heat instead of a thermometer that boils over with rising emotions. The goal is to turn stress cycles into coping cycles.[212]

Children's brains are primed to seek attachment figures in times of trouble. The very presence of trusted adults or peers serves to reduce the impact of stress.[213] Problems are a burden which is why we are anxious to have somebody help us carry them. Those who have experienced trauma or unresolved conflict are hungry to find a supportive listener. They want to tell their story and are likely to open up if the listener can establish trust and communicate in a respectful manner.[214]

Since problems pose powerful teaching opportunities, it is ironic that traditional discipline cuts off positive communication at the very time youth could benefit from such support. Some suppose that giving "attention" to youth who are misbehaving will reward problem behaviour. While such is possible, the reality is usually quite different. Providing support in moments of crisis strengthens connections and coping skills.

The best way of handling angry and upset persons is to seek to gain their voluntary compliance rather than get drawn into contests. This has become a central goal in community policing. A prominent example is "verbal judo" as developed by George Thompson, a communications professor who became a cop.[215] The Japanese word judo is a combination of *ju*, which means gentle, and *do*, which means way; so judo means the gentle way. Judo is very different from karate, which is warlike.

When Thompson first became a police officer, he got into frequent verbal confrontations with citizens because he expected to be treated with respect and would take no crap from anybody. In time he learned the power of taking crap with dignity and style. In verbal judo, if a citizen directs hostile communication at an officer, the goal is to respond with communication rather than react with force. This does not mean telling upset persons to "calm down," since such criticism implies that they have no right to be upset.

In a conflict situation, the best response is to accept the angry feelings of the other person but try to shape a positive outcome. Thus, a driver who is pulled over may angrily accuse an officer of "profiling." A verbal judo response might be, "I hear what you're saying – may I please see your license so you can get on your way." By showing empathy, one can stay calm in the midst of conflict and deflect verbal abuse. Thompson concludes, "If you cannot empathise with people, you don't stand a chance of getting them to listen to you, much less accepting your attempts to help – sincere as you may be."[216]

Adults cannot convey respect to young people by focusing on their flaws. But this deficit mindset is entrenched. Sigmund Freud is quoted as having said, "I have found little that is good about human beings. In my experience most of them are trash."[217] Such pessimism becomes a self-fulfilling prophecy. Persons respond best to those they think really like and believe in them. They respond poorly if they believe they are disliked and blamed for their problems.

In such negative encounters, self-worth is at stake.[218] Various defences are used to fend off such attacks:

- *Counterattack* fuels hostility in both parties.
- *Submission* gives a payoff for angry coercion.
- *Withdrawal* allows angry feelings to fester.
- *Disarming* the person is the most effective tactic.

Counterattack, submission, and withdrawal only serve to further jeopardise positive bonds. In contrast, disarming a person transforms the conflict into an unusual kind of cooperation. We disarm the attacker by getting out of the line of fire. One neither engages in combat nor opposes force with force. Initially we may simply ignore some interactions. It is usually helpful to join with the other, embracing the angry feelings (e.g., "I can see you are really upset.") When the person is calmer, one can express one's own needs and feelings but in a way that shows respect. In this way, tense encounters and crisis situations can be turned into opportunities to develop more positive connections.

From Conflict to Cooperation

Throughout the history of the human race, most problem-solving was a group activity. Persons formed an alliance to work cooperatively towards mutually agreed goals.[219] Such is the goal of mentoring. But mutual problem-solving cannot occur if mentors try to impose their ideas and solutions. Adolescents in particular resent directive authoritarian styles which are likely to trigger strong resistance to change.

The opposite of alliances are adversarial encounters. From an early age, children get into such contests with those in authority and they are pretty good psychologists in dealing with adults. Even before they speak, children can figure out the motivation of adults. It does not require the reasoning brain to register warmth or aloofness, attraction or repulsion, fear or security. Very young children can read subtle emotions and gauge a response. Ellen Key was one of the first to describe this ability:

> **The child, even at four or five years of age, is making experiments with adults, seeing through them, with marvellous shrewdness making his own valuations and reacting sensitively to each impression. The slightest mistrust, the smallest unkindness, the least act of injustice or contemptuous ridicule, leave wounds that last for life in the finely strung soul of the child. While on the other side, unexpected friendliness, kind advances, just indignation, make quite as deep an impression.** [220]

Charles Darwin was the first to discover that the ability to read emotions is inborn in children. He had missionaries from around the world take along photographs of persons displaying various emotions. In every tribe or culture, the same emotions were identified. Emotions are the universal language of the human race.

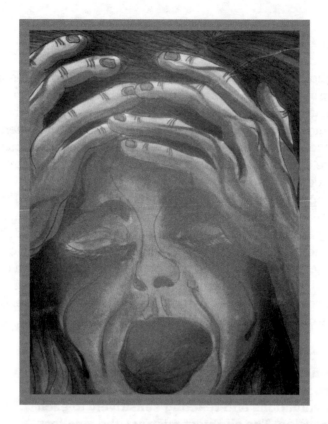

We convey emotions in facial expressions which signal the inner state of other persons. It is significant that when drawing a person, small children produce a face but few body details. They already know the most vital information for social survival is displayed by happy or distressed human faces. A second major channel for emotional information is tone of voice. Reading emotion in voice and facial expressions is the job of the amygdala.

Swiss educator Paul Diel[221] observed that verbal or nonverbal *rancour* renders any correction ineffective. Rancour is an emotionally charged communication conveying bitterness and malice. It is the prime symptom of discord in any disrupted relationship. The first step in work with families or teachers is to secure an agreement from the adult that any sign of rancour and reproach would immediately cease.

Emotional negativity stirs conflict and avoidance and undercuts efforts to be helpful.[222] Instead of speaking vaguely of the need to "build positive relationships" we can now identify the specific behaviours that create or destroy positive connections. Both mentors and youth must show respect and stop rancour in interactions with others. This includes the words one uses, the tone of voice, and perhaps most powerful, the nonverbal demeanour. Young people react to the "total package" to decide if this is a person to whom they are willing to connect.

It is difficult to continue a positive investment in those who keep resisting our bids for connection. Blanchard suggests resistant individuals are actually trying to teach us a better way to engage with them.[223] Here is a quick listing of the perceptions of youth who resist engaging with a mentor, followed by actions that serve to foster connections.

1. *I don't feel safe.* Use small interactions to build trust.
2. *You are getting close too fast.* Don't rush, respect boundaries.
3. *You think I am stupid.* Engage in a talent hunt to find strengths.
4. *Nobody understands.* Listen but don't preach or pontificate.
5. *I feel blamed and ashamed.* Never embarrass or insult.
6. *I feel like giving up.* The youth searches your face to find hope.
7. *I distrust your motives.* Be transparent and direct about your intent.
8. *These talks are boring.* Follow their interests and goals.
9. *I don't feel accepted and liked.* Be friendly, show you enjoy the youth.
10. *I am treated like an inferior.* Respect youth and share power.

If a youth's behaviour says, "I cannot connect with you," we don't take this personally but get busy figuring out how to be more helpful, responsive, and respectful. Even when discussing problems, we have opportunities to validate the positive qualities of young persons. For example, instead of asking, "Why did you do something like that?" we simply frame the question, "How did a kid like you get into trouble like that?" This implies that the youth is more than his or her behaviour.

In a fascinating study, young persons residing in group homes evaluated video clips of interactions between staff and youth.[224] They were asked to rate the behaviours of adults that they most liked and disliked. The table below summarises their ratings on a scale from 0 to 4.

Ratings of boys and girls were similar in most categories with two exceptions. Girls disliked unpleasant physical contact even more than boys. Boys disliked profanity even more than girls. The researchers were surprised to find that although joking was one of the most highly valued adult behaviours, these humorous exchanges were totally absent from actual observations of staff in these group homes for troubled youth. This list was used to train staff to use

Adult Behaviours Youth Most Desire		Adult Behaviours Youth Most Dislike	
Calm, pleasant voice	3.80	Throwing objects	0.00
Offer of help	3.70	Accusing-blaming	0.10
Joking	3.60	Shouting	0.10
Positive feedback	3.60	No opportunity to speak	0.30
Fairness	3.60	Mean, insulting remarks	0.50
Explains things	3.40		
Politeness	3.30	Unpleasant physical contact	0.60
Gets right to the point	3.10	Bad attitude	0.60
Smiling	3.00	Bossy-demanding	0.70
		Unpleasant	0.80
		Unfriendly	0.90
		Lack of understanding	1.00
		Profanity	1.00

desired behaviours leading to positive connections and to eliminate those behaviours evoking negative reactions from youth.

Canadian researchers interviewed youth about their experiences with counsellors who were trying to diagnose their problems.[225] Youth said that they do not cooperate with workers with whom they have no established connections. They resented being forced to answer questions about their personal lives and activities that they felt were intrusive and demeaning. While they resisted those who probed into their past, they were more willing to discuss challenges being faced "now and tomorrow." The researchers concluded that the most important diagnosis is made by the youth. Kids who are adult wary make a careful assessment: *Can I trust this person to help me overcome my difficulties?*

5

Coping with Challenge

In the worst of times, incredibly, that's when hope appears, like a seed, like a bulb splitting.
— Maya Angelou[226]

How do we help children and young people cope with problems and develop the strengths to surmount life challenges? A study published by the American Psychological Association called for practical methods so those who work most closely with young people can help them learn positive lessons from their problem behaviour.[227] Such skills are needed not only by professionals but by all who interact in the life space of young persons. This includes workers on the front-line, mentors in the community, parents, and young people themselves.

In this chapter we introduce a strength-building model grounded in the science of resilience and positive youth development. *Response Ability Pathways* – or RAP for short – is a program for training adult or peer mentors to support young persons as they cope with difficult challenges. RAP provides mentors with skills to *respond rather than react* to problem behaviour. RAP enables young persons to take pathways toward responsibility.[228]

Problems as Opportunities

Most children learn to cope with life's challenges through informal support rather than formal training. But some have gaps in social problem-solving skills and require more intentional teaching or treatment. Such approaches range from boot camps for "teaching discipline" to curriculums for "raising self-esteem." Concerns about discipline and school safety have sparked hundreds of violence prevention programs. Few are grounded in solid research. In spite of testimonials by proponents, such programs seldom create lasting positive change.[229] Effective interventions must be *evidence-based*, that is to say, employing principles and practices validated by solid theory and research.[230]

Among the most widely researched approaches for teaching strengths are programs for social skills training. Typically such training shows positive initial results; however, gains may not be sustained when training ends.[231] Skills taught through an artificial curriculum in artificial settings do not readily transfer to the natural environment.

While the young are very social beings, they are not motivated to stand in line to get training by adults to correct social skill deficits. Not that they don't want to solve problems, but young persons are most receptive to help offered through natural social support by trusted adults or peers. Real-life learning is more relevant than contrived lessons.[232] The most powerful interventions move problem-solving into the natural life space where difficulties are being experienced.[233] Thus, RAP focuses on the here-and-now challenges young people face in their daily lives.

A problem is a challenging situation which produces stress or "felt difficulty."[234] Our ability to deal with stress is a combination of inner strengths and external supports.[235] Walking down a dark street at night, a person trained in self-defence might feel confident, when one less equipped would be terrified. Whatever their resources, individuals are better able to cope with stress when in the company of trusted persons. An otherwise frightening situation can even be funny when we are with a group: witness the bravado of teens in a gang. But to a person without either inner strength or external support, stress becomes a crisis.[236]

Studies of large samples of children show that coping with problems is part of the normal process of growth.[237] There is no such thing as a youngster without problems. In fact children who have "too bountiful" a start may not be well-equipped to deal with inevitable life challenges. The difference between those who are seen as "seriously disturbed" and those who remain in the "normal" group is not the existence of problems but how these are handled.

Every child struggles to find solutions to problems in school and life. The outcome shapes views of self, others, and the world. Most children have a checkerboard of strengths and limitations that make them both resilient and vulnerable. If they use ineffective coping behaviour, they create problems instead of solutions to cope more effectively.[238] Children use various coping strategies:

- *First things first* – focusing on only one problem at a time.
- *Dosing challenges* – breaking hard tasks into smaller steps.
- *Working harder* – expending more effort to find a solution.
- *Tolerating frustration* – adapting to situations that cannot be changed.
- *Defensive reactions* – fight or flight behaviour and thinking distortions.

Children who learn to cope effectively develop strengths to meet future challenges. Resilient children learn to trust in their abilities and in others. They have healthy pride and can tackle the challenges of life. Fourteen-year-old Karl explained: "As you encounter one stressful experience, it strengthens you, like a vaccine, for future crisis... you have to bounce back or you couldn't go on." [239]

Children learn both by emotional conditioning and by logical problem-solving. In a classic experiment, Watson conditioned a child to fear a bunny by associating the animal with a loud noise. Thereafter, just the sight of a bunny triggered fear reactions. Such conditioned learning may last a lifetime yet operate largely outside of our conscious problem-solving brain.

Psychologists have many theories about problem-solving, some of which are very simple and understandable. A half century ago, Mowrer[240] and Piaget[241] proposed similar three-stage models for problem-solving. Any successful problem-solving must accomplish these tasks, which Piaget called "acts of intelligence": 1) identify a problem, 2) search for a solution, and 3) take purposeful action.

The human brain specialises in problem-solving. When it is finished with one problem, it seeks out another. In spite of its love for problems, the brain does not like to have uncompleted tasks in its in-box. If a person has not been able to solve a problem, the brain keeps scanning for solutions, sometimes even when we are asleep or dreaming. This inborn motivation to keep thinking about unsolved problems is called the Zeigarnik effect.[242]

The brain's tendency to keep stewing about problems provides a natural motivation for change.[243] In fact, persons with unresolved conflicts are more receptive to help and to trying new alternatives than when they are in a steady state.[244] Recall your own situation when you could not remember the name of a person whom you should know. Even after you have given up on trying to retrieve the name, the brain keeps scanning your memory bank and then the solution pops into your mind when you least expect it. Einstein had the same problem. When he figured out that existing theories of physics were wrong, he felt compelled to spend seven stressful years trying to resolve the problem of how the universe operated.[245]

The good news about the Zeigarnik effect is that if a kid has not solved some problem, there is an inborn motivation to do so. These critical events are being permanently etched into the brain's memory bank. A mentor can help provide a fresh perspective if the youth trusts enough to talk about the problem.

Powerful Life Events

Through the stories we tell, humans make meaning out of life experiences.[246] By listening to children's stories, we can discover how they think and feel, and why they act as they do. One of the first to capitalise on the power of stories was Fritz Redl who came from Austria to the United States prior to World War II.[247] Redl worked with aggressive children from Detroit. He found that traditional office-based counselling was ineffectual with angry and explosive urban youngsters.

Redl rejected the common notion of the times that *children who hate,* as he called them, would get better by acting out their angry feelings. Instead, they needed *controls from within.* While most therapists of that era tried to dig into a child's early history, Redl took a different approach. He focused on *here-and-now* problems in a child's immediate *life space.*[248]

A temper tantrum, a problem in school, conflict with peers, the illness of a parent – such critical events became the basis for teaching. Redl was one of the first to see problems as learning opportunities. He called for serious talks with children rather than severe punishments. He found that most troubled kids did not think clearly about their actions, but reacted impulsively. If asked, "why were you kicked out of class" a youngster might say "because the teacher is a shit-head." By helping the child examine what triggered this problem, and what the consequences of behaviour were, children could learn better ways to cope with challenges.[249]

Every child has stories to tell if a trusted listener can be found. Those who work most closely with young persons are in the best position to connect and engage them in these discussions. Redl's proposal was simple: ask a young person to recount to us what happened in some significant event. For example, a teacher sends a learner to the school office for some misbehaviour. By exploring what happened in this problem event, we get a snapshot of how this young person thinks, feels, and acts.

> **We get down to brass tacks. What does the child do? What does he say? What bothers you about his behaviour? What does he look like? How does it start? Where does it end?**[250]

The advantage of exploring events is that almost anybody can understand them, including young persons themselves. Even children with cognitive disabilities can communicate most clearly by relating stories of events.[251] Sticking to events avoids the trap of confusing clinical jargon. Knowing how events were experienced and interpreted gives clearer information than translating behaviour into specialised professional jargon.[252]

Many researchers now see studying events as the key to understanding human behaviour. These events are called by various labels including behavioural cycles,[253] social episodes,[254] behavioural episodes,[255] and critical incidents.[256] Events help us understand coping behaviour.[257] In recounting events, a person clarifies the timeline of action, the goal of behaviour, the related thoughts and feelings, and the consequences.

Humans are naturally motivated to talk about emotionally charged events.[258] Persons who "tell their story" reduce stress and bond with others. We cannot change past events, but we can learn from them. But youth should not be forced to disclose painful material they may not wish to reveal for the intent is not to re-open past wounds and re-traumatise a youth.[259] Likewise, adult or peer mentors who get into problems they do not feel prepared to handle should seek guidance from a trained professional. These are reasons to keep the primary focus on "here-and-now" events. We want kids to gain insight, not so much into their distant past, but into such practical questions like: How is my behaviour helping me meet my goals? How does my behaviour affect others?

The human brain uses stories to transmit complex information.[260] Yet interviewers seeking specific information often interrupt and disrupt stories. Asking questions to clarify a youth's own account keeps conversation flowing. But shifting topics without getting permission blocks communication. Probing into private matters causes threat and resistance. This is why many kids don't want to talk with counsellors.

In the natural flow of conversation, we can listen for "window words" which offer an opening for expressing interest by asking clarifying questions. An example is provided below. Lisa was sent to a counsellor because of drinking problems. Rather than immediately confronting Lisa, the counsellor allows Lisa to bring up this problem herself and thus avoids provoking resistance.[261]

Lisa: *I didn't ask to see you.*

Counsellor: *Who did ask you to see me?*

Lisa: *Don't know. Social worker, probably.*

Counsellor: *What does he think the problem is?*

Lisa: *Staying out on weekends, not knowing where I am.*

Counsellor: *So why did he ask you to come to this place?*

Lisa: *Because he thinks I drink too much.*

Counsellor: *And what do you think about your drinking?*

Lisa: *I only drink on weekends...*

Once Lisa raises the topic of drinking, this opens a window for new conversation. Lisa goes on to tell the story of how she blew all of her money in one drinking episode. The discussion revolves about drinking but Lisa doesn't object since she brought it up. As young persons share their stories, they invite us into their inner lives.

The most effective methods to change behaviour involve providing encouragement, raising questions, and helping youth clarify and reframe the problems they are facing.[262] The biggest challenge is to listen instead of trying to "fix" kids. In fact, listening is harder work than fixing.[263]

The Inside Kid

Young persons are the leading experts on their own behaviour. Alfred Adler contended that the best way to understand behaviour was to discover the goals and *private logic* beneath the action. He defined private logic as an individual's personal view of self, others, and the world:

- I am - - -
- others are - - -
- the world is - - -
- therefore - - -

This important "inside information" is often missing – even in thick case files.

Behavioural assessment tracks what happens before and after a specific behaviour. Psychologists call this sequence ABC, which stands for Antecedent, Behaviour, and Consequence. ABC is useful, but only looks at the *outside kid*. We want to connect with the *inside kid* so we can understand private logic and emotions underlying the behaviour.[264] Of course, the youth is the only one who knows what is going on in his or her private world. We do not get to private logic by asking "how do you feel?" or "what are you thinking?" Instead we engage a youth in discussing some here-and-now event.

Problem events are not isolated occurrences. Kids don't reinvent themselves every day. Instead, they keep getting into the same mistakes. These failure cycles have been called by many names: conflict cycles;[265] stress cycles;[266] argument cycles;[267] recidivism cycles;[268] coercive cycles,[269] and anger escalation.[270] Stuck in these ruts, kids don't learn from punishment. Frustrated adults keep asking the wrong question: *What kind of consequence can change this behaviour?* A better question is this: *Why does this behaviour persist in spite of negative consequences?*

When we listen to youth, we open a window to their private logic. As they describe events, a certain *thinking style* becomes apparent. This is important because the way one thinks determines how one acts. Distorted or biased thinking leads to self-defeating behaviour. John Gibbs has identified four common thinking errors behind most problem behaviour of youth.[271] These can be remembered by the letters BAMMS:

Blaming
Not taking responsibility but shifting the blame to others, or wallowing in self blame. *People always make me mad.*

Assuming the Worst
Pessimism and false beliefs that others have hostile intentions. *You can't trust anybody. People will stab you in the back.*

Minimising/**M**islabelling
Describing harmful behaviour as if it is no big deal and giving belittling labels to others. *So I hit him. He's a jerk.*

Self-centred thinking
Dwelling on one's own needs and being inconsiderate of the needs of others. *When I see something I like, I take it.*

Some thinking errors serve to protect fragile self-esteem so we don't want to steamroll over their errors in thinking. Usually by posing respectful questions, we can help a person clarify their private logic. But those with highly entrenched thinking distortions may need more focused intervention. The next chapter shows how gentle confrontation can help youth take responsibility for their behaviour instead of getting mired in self-centred thinking.

Understanding behaviour does not excuse it. We strongly believe that all hurting behaviour must stop whether it harms oneself or others. Still, kids have their reasons. Even "senseless" behaviour often makes sense when we understand a young person's sometimes confused private logic. For example, a youth who liked school kept acting out to try to get expelled. Finally a teacher discovered that the boy was living with an elderly grandmother who couldn't afford medication she needed. In the youth's private logic, if he were kicked out of school, he could support his grandmother.

Even if one cannot immediately change long-standing patterns of thinking, it is possible to help youth slow down and look at their behaviour. By considering other views than their own, they see how their actions cause problems for others. By examining their behaviour, they see that they need to take new approaches in order to meet their goals. As they share stories about challenging life events, they find new ways to cope with challenge.

Resilient Coping

While cycles of conflict, stress, anger, argument, recidivism, and coercion describe problem behaviour, we prefer a more positive term. We will speak of *coping with challenge* to keep the focus on resilience. Problems are a normal part of everybody's daily existence. Learning to manage stress and difficulty is the life curriculum for building resilience.

A youth who is overwhelmed by anger, fear, or sadness is not ready to solve problems. With extreme emotion, the brain's centres for rational thinking and positive emotions shut down.[272] Thus, in times of emotional distress, the first priority is to create a safe environment and help the youth calm feelings. Young persons need to develop the ability to reflect on their emotions instead of acting them out impulsively. Even those who have this capacity often fail to use it in the grip of intense feeling or severe stress.[273] But the good news is that the logical brain is designed for keeping reins on the emotional brain. As we think and talk about our feelings, we begin to get them under control.

With emotionally agitated young persons, the goal is to restore calm. But we need to honour their feelings and not tell them they should not be upset.[274] Youngsters feel disconnected if we maintain a deadpan calm and do not seem to notice their pain. Therefore, we respond to children's feelings by showing genuine concern, by joining with them in their moment of pain. If the feeling is positive, we can join in that as well.

Kids in conflict are caged in painful emotions. Providing support de-escalates angry emotions. Leaving the person alone to cool off works with some kids, but with others it can also fuel fury and alienation.[275] We build supportive bonds by being there in time of crisis and walking through the storm.

The only antidote to negative emotions is to arouse positive emotions. Brain research shows the most prevalent positive emotions in humans to be *social interest* and *curiosity*. We are most productive and creative when operating in this problem-solving mode called "flow."[276] The desire to connect with others and cope with challenges is the normal state of affairs in healthy children who are not overwhelmed by threat. People who show curiosity and interest are likely to find this reciprocated.

CLEAR Thinking

We use a timeline for assessing behaviour which studies not only actions but also the young person's private logic and motivations. Brain research shows that humans cope with stressful events in predictable ways. **C**hallenge registers in **L**ogic and **E**motions causing **A**ctions that lead to **R**esults. We call this coping cycle **CLEAR**.

Challenge
An external or internal event triggers stress or "felt difficulty." Challenges are tests of one's abilities or resources to cope with difficulty. These range from minor distractions to major disruptions posing either threat or opportunity. Challenges are detected by the brain's sentry, the Amygdala.

Logic
This involves perception, thinking, and language. Each individual develops a unique style of private logic drawing from personal experiences as well as innate brain-based programs. This private logic is used to make sense of the world and plan actions to meet desired goals. Logic and reasoning are managed by the higher problem-solving centres of the human brain.

Emotions
Emotions motivate, propelling a person toward some preprogrammed action, such as befriending or attacking another person. The words *emotion* and *motivation* come from the same root word, "move." Without control from the logical brain, emotions lead to impulsive reactions. The emotional brain also connects to the "reptilian brain" which governs reflexive fight-flight reactions.

Actions
Behaviour is directed towards some goal. All behaviour serves some purpose, whether or not it "makes sense" to the individual or outside observers. Behaviour may be pro-social or anti-social and self-defeating. Behavioural actions are influenced by both the emotional and logical brain.

Results
These are consequences of behavioural actions. They can be *observable*, such as the reactions of others, as well as *private* thoughts and feelings, such as "I like hurting other people." Even punished behaviour may be reinforced if it makes sense in a person's private logic. As problems are resolved, the brain is calmed. Unsolved problems trigger new conflict and cycles of coping.

We seek CLEAR thinking about some event by exploring this time-line. While we don't force youth to report on this sequence in the exact way it occurred, at the end of the conversation we should have a pretty good idea about important facts at each stage. What initial event triggered stress or challenge? What was the person's private logic? What were the emotions motivating action? What action did the person take? What was the result?

We will want to make sure of the details of exactly what happened. Kids in conflict do not think in logical, sequential ways, and sometimes they seek to obscure what really happens. But, as we clarify events and thinking, youth can see how others view their behaviour and whether their actions are achieving their goals. These are broad guidelines, and the more natural the flow of conversation, the better.

Two persons are putting their minds together to try to understand some problem. Of course, if the problem is too serious, formal counselling can follow. But research shows that even very troubled persons can gain valuable insight by talking with trusted adults or peers in their natural setting.[277] This has some advantages over traditional office-based assessment where youth have to connect with persons who may not know them well or understand the background of the problem.

It does little good to label kids who get in conflict as "trouble makers" any more than a doctor would call their patients "illness makers." Troubled young people are trying to cope in ways that cause more pain to self and others.[278] They need to learn how to deal with challenges in mature and responsible ways. This is the goal of RAP.

RAP Basics

As we have seen, RAP is a method for adults or peers to provide positive support to young persons in both good times and in difficulty. RAP uses natural moment-by-moment interactions as the basis for growth. RAP may involve verbal dialogue or non-verbal exchanges. RAP can be used to resolve a conflict or RAP can prevent conflict through small dosages of encouragement.

If the occasion arises to discuss a problem, RAP provides a guide for clarifying the nature of the difficulty and finding a responsible solution. RAP dialogues are not limited to discussing problems but also highlight strengths and help youth develop positive goals. In all cases, RAP is designed to build resilience *by responding to the young person's needs* for belonging, mastery, independence, and generosity.

RAP includes three different interventions: Connecting, Clarifying, and Restoring. These are landmarks on the roadmap for solving problems and putting kids on new pathways. Together, they form a logical sequence:

- *Connecting* in order to provide support;
- *Clarifying* problems and possible solutions;
- *Restoring* harmony and social bonds. These processes are described below.

Connecting, clarifying, and restoring are all normal self-corrective processes. We all do these things our entire life, some of us better than others. Thus, RAP is a natural, intuitive way to strengthen capacity that kids already have to build positive bonds, make sense of challenges, and put relationships back in balance.

While connect, clarify, and restore is the natural sequence of RAP, these steps can also be used as separate interventions. It is not always possible or necessary to follow all RAP stages since each is a positive initiative in its own right:

Connect

Connections are *natural emotional bonds* that motivate persons to be positive and respectful. This alone may solve many problems without further intervention. School-based research shows that when adversarial climates are replaced with cooperation, discipline problems decline and achievement soars.[279] Not all connections are time-intensive. In some cases, one can make a positive connection in seconds, even if the young person is in a larger group. A teacher in a classroom has hundreds of opportunities each day to provide small doses of encouragement and affirmation on the side, even as formal lessons occupy centre stage.

Clarify

By giving persons the opportunity to reflect on challenges and think clearly, we support *natural problem-solving*. With better understanding of a situation, fresh solutions may emerge. Some difficulties are dilemmas rather than problems, since no easy solution is available. A twelve-year-old boy who is struggling with the reality of a parent dying of AIDS has no remedy at hand. But by talking about this difficulty, he is able to manage his emotions and cope more effectively.

Restore

Resolving conflicts and meeting needs creates natural harmony and healing. The goal is to build strengths and provide supports to help young persons meet important goals. But one does not need to come up with a life-altering plan. Often, by identifying at least one action a young person can take, and one support others can provide, we put the young person on the first steps of a restorative pathway.

Since RAP is an application of natural interpersonal abilities, it can be used in a wide range of settings by both adult and youth mentors. While RAP can be "therapeutic," it is not designed to replace therapy.[280] While RAP is "educational," it does not impose a formal curriculum. RAP is really "mentoring for resilience." Since the goal is to build strengths in youth, the young person is as much an expert as is the adult or peer mentor.

RAP is a targeted intervention geared to bring immediate payoffs. RAP can provide as much support as the "teaching moment" allows, whether literally a moment or an hour or days. Sometimes several very short RAP interactions spread over time are better than an intensive session. Distrustful young persons are in a conflict about whether to approach or retreat, and short positive connections without a lot of conversation may be less threatening.

Teachers tell us that they feel frustrated that they have so little time to spend with certain young persons whose needs are so great. But resilience studies show that one person can make a big difference, sometimes even with a single act of kindness.[281] A small, carefully targeted effort can become a *tipping point* that alters the pathway of an individual's life.[282] These brief encounters can be potent because they focus on a specific goal and motivate the person to change the direction of their behaviour.[283] RAP has an economy of efficiency. Like a laser, it targets a specific challenge and spotlights strengths. As seen in the following example, even a single encounter can have a real impact.

A RAP in Action

To demonstrate RAP in action, we share this story which involves a youth from Canada. This account was provided by an editor of the *Reclaiming Children and Youth* journal who was speaking to a gathering of youth professionals.

"Before my luncheon address , a short speech was given by a youth in care named Jonathan. His topic was, *The Person Behind the File Number*. His sobering theme was that – in his experience – most professionals don't really listen to kids but just treat them as cases to be managed. Though he clearly didn't trust adults much, he made his points with genuineness and his address was well received.

"During my address on the topic of resilience, I noticed that Jonathan was intensely interested in my examples of young persons who had surmounted great difficulties. Though Jonathan was fifty feet back in the audience, I occasionally made brief eye contact with him without making this obvious to others in attendance. For example, speaking of "hidden greatness in every young person," Jonathan and I locked eyes for a second or two. Soon Jonathan was hanging on every word.

"After the speech, Jonathan was eagerly waiting near the door. He surprised me by making a bid for further communication: 'I don't have anything to do this afternoon if you have time to talk.' Soon we were sitting in the corner of the hotel lobby. Without prodding Jonathan began to recount his life story. He was removed from his parents as a young boy, and had spent several years in care facilities. In spite of adversity, Jonathan displayed remarkable resilient behaviour. With humour and insight, Jonathan shared what it was like to grow up as 'property of the government' and to have no voice concerning his destiny.

"My inclination is to talk about the present and future, but Jonathan seemed to want to talk about unhealed wounds. As he became more comfortable, his humour gave way to sadness. Then he opened a window into his private world by saying, 'I never told anybody this before but I sometimes wish I could disappear and go somewhere where I could start my life over. *Since I was four, I haven't had any good memories.*'

"These were window words and Jonathan was inviting me to share his pain. 'What happened back then to make you so unhappy?' I asked.

"Jonathan plunged into his pain of all pains. He told of being with his Dad at age four and watching him shoot himself. 'I blamed myself for my Dad's death, but I didn't say anything about this. I have always wondered that maybe I had done something to make him kill himself. I can't figure out if I was not a good kid and caused him trouble. I would have nightmares, but I didn't want to tell anybody. Even though it's a bad memory, it's my only memory of my Dad, so if I shared it with anyone, it would not be my own.'

"I told him how much courage he had to talk about things that had bothered him all these years. I said it is normal for any little kid to blame himself when something goes terribly wrong and they lose someone they love. I assured him that now that he is more mature, he will begin to realise that he couldn't possibly have had anything to do with his dad's death. He seemed greatly reassured and conversation turned to other topics.

"Jonathan penned some of the ideas we talked about as additions to his speech, which was published in the journal *Reclaiming Children and Youth*. This is a young man who has known much pain but who is learning to connect with others, surmount past problems, and plan for the future."

We close this chapter with excerpts from Jonathan's speech. A young veteran of the care system gives advice to those working with young people in pain:

I know you are all busy – lots of work that demands paper, paper, paper. But I am here to tell you that I am more than a file. I am a person. I have feelings and am entitled to respect. Please don't only see the problems, see the potential. Over the years, I have had good and bad experiences in the system. The good parts have been some of the caring, trusting, and supportive people I have come in contact with. The bad parts are when people don't listen or trust me.

I check out people very carefully. I am good at reading people. Sometimes I use reverse psychology, like if a counsellor is getting too close, then I ask him about his life, his problems, and it scares him away. I can tell if a person really cares and wants to help or is just doing a job for the money.

If I find a person who is open, his personality reaches my own and I bond quickly. But I don't want to talk about things that hurt. After being somebody who doesn't care about anything for so many years, it is hard to change.

I still find it hard to trust anybody except myself, but my life is now starting to turn around. I am in a supervised independent living program and am working and completing high school. I am working as a chef in training. Someday I would like to be a chef on a cruise ship, as one of my other interests is marine biology. I also enjoy boxing.

For kids like me in the system, there is a lot of fear. Most kids I know don't want to talk about their problems or experiences because it will cause them more trouble. Adults need to build a bond with kids and then they will tell you if they are ready.

Sometimes workers lose sight of the person behind the file number. I have desires and goals, and it is important to be there in helping me achieve my potential. Some people clear the way for me and others put up roadblocks. I am the best resource you have to know and understand what is going on inside of me. [284]

6

Restoring Respect

Let us build communities and families in which our children and youth, especially those who are most troubled, can belong. Let us build a country in which our children and youth can learn to care for and respect others so that one day they, too, will build a family, a community, and a country which is well and strong.
— Nelson Mandela[285]

Nelson Mandela once said, "There can be no keener revelation of a society's soul than the way it treats its children."[286] When young people feel respected, they have no reason to be disrespectful to adults or peers. Plato (427-347 BC) believed that teaching children to live in harmony and respect was more important than giving them riches. But he cautioned that respect cannot be taught by reprimand, but only by "lifelong visible practice" that models the behaviour and values we hope to teach.

Children don't learn respect by obedience training but by being treated with respect. The word respect is equivalent of the Golden Rule. In Latin *re* means to give back, as in treating the other person as you would want to be treated under those conditions, even if the person does not seem to deserve respect. Empathy and fairness are the foundations of character and moral development. The opposite is egotism, being self-centred and ignoring the needs of others.[287]

Concern for others does not mean ignoring one's own needs. As Desmond Tutu observed, if we don't respect ourselves, we are likely to show it by being disrespectful to others.[288] But even when dealing with adversaries, reconciliation and restoring social bonds is the pathway to harmony.

Restoring Social Bonds

How should a society, a community, or a group respond when its members cause pain and harm to one another? This question is as old as human experience and only two answers have arisen:

- *Those who hurt others must be made to suffer;* this is the definition of justice in dominator cultures. Reinforcing this principle is the human brain, which is hard-wired for retribution.
- *Those who hurt others must restore their broken bonds;* this is the type of justice practised in communities that treat all members as relatives. This restorative principle gains support from many great spiritual traditions.[289]

While restorative approaches are also grounded in scientific evidence and practice wisdom, how we treat others ultimately comes down to a question of values. A leader in restorative approaches contends the core value that must govern our approach to human conflict is respect, even for those who are different or are seen as enemies.[290] The value of respect demands that we respond to the needs of all, those who are hurt as well as those who harm others. All need healing.

Young people need to understand the consequences their actions have on others. This requires teaching them to respect others and mend broken bonds. The core value of the community becomes: *No one has the right to hurt themselves or others and everyone has the responsibility to help.*

In a society where alienation between children and adults is widespread, many youth seek out other adult-detached peers to meet their needs. Weakly bonded to family or school, they form negative youth subcultures and become trapped in self-centred, exploitative lifestyles. Angry and lacking hope and purpose, they neither respect themselves nor treat others respectfully. They desperately need prosocial modelling and values from caring adults and peers. Instead, their antisocial behaviour often results only in punishment and exclusion, which further weakens their social bonds.

By their actions, young people in conflict can destroy connections with their peers, caregivers, or teachers. A fight in a classroom may result in the student being excluded from future classes or avoiding school the next day. An argument between a caregiver and a child may result in tension and inability to continue relating. An act of violence against a community member may result in rejection from family and community.

When connections are broken, even for short periods of time, the pain experienced by all parties calls for restoration. Young people need encouragement and support to restore bonds as soon as possible. Prolonged disconnections create alienation, fuel animosity, and cause further conflict and rejection.

Creating respectful relationships often requires a fundamental change in the values and thinking patterns that have caused youths to hurt themselves or others. Underlying these expectations is a belief that even highly troubled youths have strengths and potentials, and that they are able to assume responsibility for their lives and make positive contributions to others. This involves specific techniques for reversing responsibility, confronting with concern, fostering a spirit of service, and helping youth find purpose.[291]

Reversing Responsibility

Children do not develop responsibility by being turned loose without limits. Adults who just try to nurture but don't set behavioural expectations seldom have strong influence. Youth may see them as weak and they become "friends without influence." On the other hand, "get tough" dictatorial adults who demand absolute obedience are equally ineffective.[292] The trick is to navigate between these extremes, able to nurture *and* set high expectations. This involves demanding responsibility instead of obedience.

Youth who are experiencing problems need to take responsibility for their own behaviour. Psychologists call this "self-efficacy," and it means taking control of one's life and one's actions. But many youth (and adults) are accustomed to blaming their own difficulties on others or to retreating in helplessness.

The tendency to shift responsibility elsewhere for one's problems is a fine art with many children. Blaming parents or principals or police eliminates motivation to honestly face up to problems and change the course of one's life. Since many youth are good at putting off responsibility, mentors must be more skilful at reversing responsibility. This is done with simple verbal interactions, such as the following:

Youth shifts responsibility:
Why should I care? Nobody cares about me.

Mentor reverses responsibility:
Then perhaps it's up to you to take charge of your own life.

Reversing responsibility can also be done in a group setting which can serve to build a norm of taking responsibility among all members of the group:

Youth shifts responsibility:
What do you expect? My parents are both drunks.

Mentor reverses responsibility:
Is Tony trying to tell the group that everybody with alcoholic parents decides to abuse alcohol?

The goal is not to become embroiled in an argument, but rather to communicate in a simple, respectful way that we believe the youth is mature enough to assume responsibility for self. This does not mean we cannot express empathy for a youth who has been hurt but we do not encourage the victim status.

As the technique of reversing responsibility is modelled, young people will begin to use it with irresponsible peers. Reversal is a special case of respectful confrontation. As one youth said of this technique, "It's like they hold up a mirror; and whatever the problem is, you find the answer to it somewhere inside of yourself!"

Confronting with Concern

The word *confront* can be confusing since it has two possible definitions. It can mean to attack, as to confront in battle. It also means to face something directly, like confronting a problem. The latter definition applies to our discussion.

Any behaviours that pose harm to self and others are considered to be problems in need of solution. Persons who are comfortable with hurtful behaviour are unlikely to change unless the reality of what they are doing becomes very clear. Most suffer not from excess guilt, but from a lack of it. Only when they understand how they have hurt themselves and others with their actions will they be motivated to change.

Confrontation rooted in animosity or indifference will not have a positive result. In fact, hostile, demeaning confrontation (attacking the person, not the behaviour) will quickly destroy positive bonds. On the other hand, there is no more powerful method of discipline than to be kindly confronted by persons who deeply care about you.

Young people cannot benefit from criticism unless it is balanced with positive encouragement. According to research at Girls and Boys Town, this requires a ratio of support to criticism of 9 to 1. One useful way of delivering correction is to "sandwich" a constructive critique between two supportive messages. For example:

Support: *Maria, you are really a powerful helper to your group.*

Critique: *Sometimes you forget and ridicule girls who act immature.*

Support: *They look up to you and can learn a lot from your maturity.*

Youths need to learn to deal with someone who is angry with them without either shrinking or counterattacking. Role playing, particularly with immature youths who lack assertive skills, is another means of learning to receive criticism and to express complaints. Youth learn to listen openly and actively, to express understanding of the other person's feeling and thinking, and to acknowledge areas of agreement and honest disagreement.[293]

It is sometimes necessary to respectfully challenge thinking used to justify negative behaviour. For example, youth often mislabel destructive behaviour with words such as strong, cool, smart, or sophisticated. Mentors can use a technique called reframing so that helping others becomes an instance of strength and maturity. Instead of attacking a individual's show of strength ("you aren't as strong as you think"), the mentor links strength to helping: "A person as strong as you will really be able to become a great example. Helping takes strength." Following are other examples of reframing:

- If truancy has an exciting quality, we could reframe it as immature, perhaps "playing games of hide and seek."
- If stealing is seen as "slick," it could be reframed as "sneaky and dumb."

Again, the attempt must be to confront destructive thinking and behaviour, but not attack the person. The message must come through as "this is a very immature way of acting for someone as mature as you." By pairing positive statements that recognise the dignity of a person with frank statements about behaviour and thinking errors, we communicate more powerfully without engendering resistance.

A Spirit of Service

The spirit of generosity has been noticeably missing from traditional psychology which assumes persons operate only on self-interest. This is an intriguing oversight because the call to show concern for the needs of others is a foundation principle of the world's great ethical systems.

Caring is not fashionable among many youth. Young persons must tame their self-centred bias and become as concerned for others as for themselves. A person without empathy has an immature character and displays behaviour that is selfish, disloyal, and narcissistic.

In coercive climates, young persons are devoid of positive relationships and role models. They bond with other marginal peers and engage in *deviance training*, supporting one another in anti-social thinking and behaviour.[294] Preventing destructive peer influence is a major challenge when problem kids are segregated from those who are more stable, as in residential care or alternative schools.[295] The best way to reverse this process is to get them hooked on helping.

The involvement of idealistic young people in service-learning is a natural match between their innate need to be of value to others and the pressing needs of our society. Yet some schools and traditional youth organizations have failed to recognise that troubled adolescents have strong needs for service and have much to offer.

At Starr Commonwealth, serving troubled youth in Michigan, students carry out more than 100 community service projects each year. Some are short term while others last many months. Among the projects have been the following:

- Serving as teacher aides at a community day care centre;
- Operating summer recreation programs for neighbourhood children;
- Assisting with Special Olympic events;
- Working with disabled children in a horse-back riding program;
- Earning money to provide food for a needy family;
- Chopping firewood for the disabled;
- Painting houses for elderly citizens.

Many modern youth feel that their presence makes little difference in the world, that they have little real control over their lives. Their irresponsibility is closely related to feelings of being helpless victims of luck, fate, or the whims of powerful others. Involvement in service-learning experiences can challenge these assumptions that they are worthless and that their actions do not matter.

Yet service-learning programs must surmount a formidable obstacle. The youth who most need to develop concern for others are notoriously self-centred. They may ridicule values of service or giving of self to others. Instead they place a premium on toughness, autonomy, daring, and the ability to exploit others. Always needing to appear strong, they are vulnerable to criticism from peers if they should show their gentler, more positive side. To overcome egocentrism, youth must be committed to something beyond themselves.

Service-learning programs can capture the commitment of troubled teenagers by appealing to their positive potentials. For example, many are more receptive to approaches that reinforce their maturity ("You can be of real help to these people") than those that maintain their dependence ("This will help you with your problems"). Helping others needs to be seen as an act of strength ("This will be a tough job") rather than weakness ("This will be easy.")

Service projects also must be seen as exciting and spontaneous rather than routine and regimented. Pioneer social worker Jane Addams observed that many youth get into trouble because of strong appetites for excitement and adventure. Highly adventurous projects may be rare, but it is possible to avoid repetitive, non-challenging helping projects. By involvement in rich and meaningful service, young persons find they can make positive contributions to the world.

Purpose and Hope

When youth become committed to prosocial roles, this can lead to a soul-searching transformation in their lives. Youth begin to ask questions of the most basic existential nature: What kind of person do I want to be? What impact do I want to have on others and the world? What do I want my life to amount to? Here is an entry from a journal written by seventeen-year-old Tyrone. He wrote this during a period of serious reflection about the meaning of his life while locked in a correctional facility:

> **A lot of times I think I'm dead. You might as well say I am. The only difference in being dead is I feel I would be a lot better off at times. Not having to worry about going out and hurting someone. Getting into trouble, even to the point of getting locked up. A lot of time I don't even know why God put me on the earth. I don't feel like I've accomplished anything but hurting people.**

Reacting to inner pain, young people such as Tyrone are in desperate need of opportunities to discover purpose in their lives. The hunger to be of value to others is seen in this final notation from Tyrone's journal. Now, no longer preoccupied with his own pain, he is starting to reach out to help others and reconstruct his life:

> **Something I would like to do is to be able to go and talk to young kids who want to run around with gangs and guns, steal, disobey their parents, or just skip school. I would like to talk to some of the kids before it gets too late and they end up where I am right now. I feel I can do a lot for them. I feel like I've done enough to some kids in the negative way, and I'd like to do some positive for them.**

Young persons need to break free from self-preoccupation and restore damaged relationships. Their natural motivation to help others can flower in environments where all treat one another with respect. By reaching out to others, young people find proof of their worth, for they are now of value.

Too often, preoccupation with problems has blinded us to strengths and potentials in young people. But in the face of today's difficulties, we can reclaim timeless wisdom. Over the millenniums, people in kinship cultures created networks of human connections in communities that reared courageous, responsible kids. Now modern research has validated this traditional wisdom. We can get back to basics by restoring bonds of respect and living in harmony with all who share our small world.

Research Notes

Introduction

1 RAP follows principles of universal design in order to be relevant to a wide range of individuals and settings. See: Scott, S., McGuire, J., & Shaw, S. (2003). Universal design for instruction. *Remedial and Special Education, 24(6)*, 369-379.

2 A mentor is a person who guides, models, teaches, or encourages a young person in a responsive, caring relationship. Both adults and responsible peers can serve in this role. See: McCluskey, K., & Mays, A. (2003), *Mentoring for talent development.* Sioux Falls, SD: Reclaiming Youth International.

3 Brendtro, L., Brokenleg, M., & Van Bockern, S. (2002). *Reclaiming youth at risk: Our hope for the future* (Rev. ed,). Bloomington, IN: National Educational Service.

4 Hillman, J. (1996). *The soul's code: In search of character and calling.* New York: Random House.

5 Courtenay, B. (1989). *The power of one*. Camberwell, Victoria, Australia: Penguin Books.

Chapter 1

6 National Film Board of Canada. (1987). *Richard Cardinal: Cry from the diary of a Métis child* [video]. Montreal, Quebec: Author.

7 National Film Board of Canada. (1987). *Richard Cardinal: Cry from a diary of a Métis child.* [video]. Montreal, Quebec: Author.

8 Davis, L. (1987). *Rivers of pain, bridges of hope*. Hong Kong: Writer's and Publisher's Cooperative.

9 Slaby, A., & Garfinkel, L., (1994). *No one saw my pain*. New York: W. W. Norton.

10 Raychaba, B. (1993). *Pain, lots of pain: Violence and abuse in the lives of young people in care.* Ottawa, ON: National Youth in Care Network.

11 Anglin, J. (2003). *Pain, normality, and the struggle for congruence: reinterpreting residential care for children and youth.* Binghamton, NY: Haworth Press, p. 111.

12 Greenspan, S. I. (1997). *The growth of the mind and the endangered origins of intelligence.* Cambridge, MA: Perseus Books, p. 49.

13 Greenspan, S. I. (1997). *The growth of the mind and the endangered origins of intelligence.* Cambridge, MA: Perseus Books, p. 25.

14 Benson, E. (2003). Researchers are still looking for consensus on how and when anger first appears in infants. *Monitor on Psychology, 34*(3), 50-51.

15 Menninger, K. (1963). *The vital balance.* New York: The Viking Press.

16 Psychologist Anatol Rapaport discovered the "tit for tat" rule in a computer simulation of human conflict. Rapaport, A. (1960). *Fights, games, and debates.* Ann Arbor, MI: University of Michigan Press.

17 Winnicott, D. (1965). *The maturational process and the facilitating environment: Studies in the theory of emotional development.* New York: International Universities Press.

18 Long, N., Wood, M., & Fecser, F. (2001). *Life space crisis intervention.* Austin, TX: PRO-ED.

19 Amygdala is pronounced ah mig' duh la. Aggleton, John P. (Ed,), (2000). *The amygdala: A functional analysis.* Oxford, UK: Oxford University Press.

20 In extreme trauma, stress can be so overwhelming that the brain switches course and acts to block the memory.

21 Eisenberger, N., Lieberman, M. & Williams. K. (2003).The pain of social exclusion. *Science, 302,* 290-292.

22 This region is the anterior singulate, which is closely tied to the amygdala in assigning an emotional valence to stimuli and determining emotional reactions.

23 Leary, M. L. (1999). The social and psychological importance of self esteem. In Robin M. Kowalski & Mark R. Leary, *The social psychology of emotional and behavioral problems* (pp. 197-221). Washington, DC: American Psychological Association.

24 The brain's ability to detect signs of rejection and inclusion has been called the sociometer. Leary, M. L. (1999). The social and psychological importance of self esteem. In Robin M. Kowalski & Mark R. Leary, *The social psychology of emotional and behavioral problems* (pp. 197-221). Washington, DC: American Psychological Association.

25 Nathanson, D. L. (1992). *Shame and pride: Affect, sex, and the birth of self.* New York: W.W. Norton.

26 Tangney, J. & Salovey, P. (1999). Problematic social emotions: Shame, guilt, jealousy, and envy. In Robin M. Kowalski & Mark R. Leary, *The social psychology of emotional and behavioral problems* (pp. 167-195). Washington, DC: American Psychological Association.

27 Garbarino, J. (1999). *Lost boys.* New York: Free Press.

28 Beck, A. (1999). *Prisoners of hate: The cognitive basis of anger, hostility, and violence.* New York: Harper Collins.

29 Raychaba, B. (1993). *Pain, lots of pain: Violence and abuse in the lives of young people in care.* Ottawa, Canada: National Youth in Care Network, p. 94.

30 Zillmann, D. (1993). Mental control of angry aggression. In D. Wegner & J. Pennebaker (Eds.) *Handbook of mental control* (pp. 370-392). Upper Saddle River, NJ: Prentice-Hall.

31 Beck, A. (1999). *Prisoners of hate: The cognitive basis of anger, hostility, and violence.* New York: Harper Collins.

32 Waller, J. (2002). *Becoming evil: How ordinary people commit genocide and mass killing.* New York: Oxford University Press.

33 Milgram, S. (1974). *Obedience to authority.* New York: Harper & Row.

34 Waller, J. (2002). *Becoming evil: How ordinary people commit genocide and mass killing.* New York: Oxford University Press.

35 According to Milgram (1974), submitting to peers or authority triggers "major alterations in the logic system" (p. 134). See: Milgram, S. (1974). *Obedience to authority.* New York: Harper & Row.

36 The tendency of normal persons to become cruel in coercive group situations is described with visual images on Philip Zinbardo's website at www.prisonexp.org For a theoretical discussion see: Zinbardo, P. G., Maslach, C., & Haney, C. (2000). *Reflections on the Stanford prison experiment: Genesis, transformations, consequences.* In T. Blass (Ed.), *Obedience to authority: Current perspectives on the Milgram paradigm* (pp. 193-237). Mahwah, NJ: Erlbaum.

37 Niehoff, D. (1999). *The biology of violence.* New York: Free Press,

38 Nichols, P. (2004). No disposable kids: A developmental look at disposability. *Reclaiming Children and Youth 13*(1), 5-11.

39 Guindon, M. H., Green, A. G., & Hanna, F. J. (2003). Intolerance and psychopathology: Toward a general diagnosis for racism, sexism, and homophobia. *American Journal of Orthopsychiatry, 73*(2), 167-176.

40 Lazarus, R., & Folkman, S. (1984). *Stress, appraisal, and coping.* New York: Springer.

41 Barber, B. (Ed.). (2002). *Intrusive parenting.* Washington, DC: American Psychological Association.

42 Parese, S. (1999). Understanding the impact of personal crisis on school performance in troubled youth. *Reclaiming Children and Youth, 8*(3), 181-187.

43 Whalen, R., & Kauffman, J. (1999). *Educating children with emotional and behavioral disorders.* Reston, VA: Council for Exceptional Children.

44 Donovan, J., Jesser, R., & Costa, S. (1988). Syndrome of problem behavior in adolescents. A replication. *Journal of Consulting and Clinical Psychology, 56,* 762-765.

45 Healy, W., & Bronner, A. (1936). *New light on delinquency and its treatment.* New Haven, CT: Yale University Press, p, 121. This classic study at Yale University compared delinquent boys with their non-delinquent brothers. Although from the same family, delinquents were seven times more likely to report severe emotional stress than their siblings.

46 Reid, J., Patterson, G., & Snyder, J. (Eds.), (2002). *Antisocial behavior in children and adolescents.* Washington, DC: American Psychological Association.

47 Rosenberg, M. (1999). *Nonviolent communication.* Encinitas, CA: Puddle Dancer Press.

48 Adler, A. (1930). *Die seele des schwererzeihbaren schulkindes.* English translation, 1963, *The Problem Child.* New York: G. P. Putnam's Sons.

49 Tillich, P. (1952). *The courage to be.* New Haven, CT: Yale University Press.

50 Brendtro, L., Brokenleg, M., & Van Bockern, S, (2002). *Reclaiming youth at risk: Our hope for the future* (Rev. ed.), Bloomington, IN: National Educational Service, (originally published 1990).

51 Vilakazi, H. (1993). Rediscovering lost truths. *Journal of Emotional and Behavioral Problems, 1*(4),37.

52 Eisler, R. (1987). *The chalice and the blade: Our history, our future.* San Francisco: HarperCollins.

53 de Mause, L. (1974). *The history of childhood.* New York: The Psychohistory Press.

54 Giago, T. (1978). *The aboriginal sin: Reflections on the Holy Rosary Indian Mission School (Red Cloud Indian School).* San Francisco: Indian Historian.

55 Pilkington, D. (2002). *Rabbit-proof fence.* New York: Miramax Books.

56 Adler, M. (1985). *Ten philosophical mistakes.* New York: Macmillan.

57 Maslow, A. (1970). *Motivation and personality* (Rev. ed.). New York: Harper & Row.

Chapter 2

58 Machel, G. (2003). Tangible care. In Nelson Mandela, *From Freedom to the future* (pp. 411-414). Johannesburg: Jonathan Ball Publishers, p. 411.

59 Durkheim, E. (1972). *Emile Durkheim: Selected writings.* Edited by Anthony Giddens. Cambridge, UK: Cambridge University Press.

60 Eisler, R. (1987). *The chalice and the blade: Our history, our future.* San Francisco: Harper Collins.

61 Wachtel, T, (2003). Restorative justice in everyday life: Beyond the formal ritual. *Reclaiming Children and Youth 12*(2), 83-87.

62 Knitzer, J., Steinberg, Z. & Fleisch, B. (1990). *At the schoolhouse door: An examination of programs and policies for children with behavioral and emotional problems.* New York: Bank Street College of Education.

63 Long, N. (1995). Why adults strike back. *Reclaiming Children and Youth,* 4(1), 11-15.

64 Wood, F, H. (1988). Factors in intervention choice. Monograph in *Behavioral Disorders, 11,*133-143. Arizona State University and Council for Children with Behavioral Disorders.

65 Parks, A. (2002). *An American GULAG: Secret POW camps for teens.* Eldorado Springs, CO: The Education Exchange.

66 Roberts, M. (2001). *Horse sense for people.* New York: Viking Press.

67 Skinner, B. F. (1948). *Walden II.* New York: Macmillan.

68 This discussion draws from a policy analysis presented by Larry Brendtro with discussion by Charles Curie of the Substance Abuse and Mental Health Services Administration to a conference of the Alliance for Children and Families, Naples, Florida, January 16, 2004. The Alliance represents non-profit children's services in the United States. See: Brendtro, L. (2004). Rethinking coercive interventions with troubled youth: Harmonizing values, research, and practice. A paper presented to the Alliance for Children and Families conference, Naples, Florida, January 16, 2004.

69 Hyman, I. (1997). *School discipline and school violence.* Boston: Allyn and Bacon.

70 Artz, S. (1998). *Sex, power, & the violent school girl.* New York: Columbia University Press.

71 Hyman, I., & Snook, P. (2001). Dangerous schools, alienated students. *Reclaiming Children and Youth, 10*(3), 133-136.

72 Garbarino, J., & de Lara, E. (2002). *And words can hurt forever: How to protect adolescents from bullying, harassment, and emotional violence.* New York: Free Press, p. 77.

73 Bettelheim, B. (1974). *A home for the heart.* London: Thames and Hudson.

74 Personal observation is by the author (LB) who toured the program immediately after it had been closed and destroyed by the students. This outcome was never discussed in the reports documenting how the program created positive behaviour change. While this program was closed in the sixties, it was cited as a model for other token economies in youth institutions.

75 Raychaba, B. (1993). *Pain, lots of pain: Violence and abuse in the lives of young people in care.* Ottawa, Canada: National Youth in Care Network, p. 88.

76 Jones, R., & Timbers, G. (2002). An analysis of the restraint event and its behavioral effects on clients and staff. *Reclaiming Children and Youth, 11*(1), 37-41.

77 Center, D. B., & Calloway, J. M, (1999). Self-reported job stress and personality in teachers of students with emotional or behavioral disorders. *Behavioral Disorders, 25*(1), 41-51.

78 Barnett, S. dos Reis, S., Riddle, M, & the Maryland Youth Practice Improvement Committee for Mental Health. (2002). Improving the management of acute aggression in state residential and inpatient psychiatric facilities for youths. *Child and Adolescent Psychiatry, 41*(8), 897-905.

79 For a discussion of destructive psychological effects of seclusion, see: Villa, D. (1986). The management of misbehavior by seclusion. *Residential Treatment of Children and Youth, 4*, 63-73. The risks of restraint, injury, or death are discussed in: Crisis Prevention Institute. (2001). Protecting kids in restraint. *Reclaiming Children and Youth, 10*(2), 162-163.

80 Viscott, David. (1996). *Emotional resilience.* New York: Crown Publishers.

81 Arnold, M. B. (1960). *Emotion and personality.* 2 volumes. New York: Columbia University Press, p. 177.

82 Kozart, M. (2002). Understanding efficacy and psychotherapy: An ethnomethodological perspective on the therapeutic alliance. *American Journal of Orthopsychiatry, 72*(2), 217-231.

83 Brendtro, L., & Shahbazian, M. (2004). *Troubled children and youth: Turning problems into opportunity.* Champaign, IL: Research Press, pp. 190-191.

84 Sells, S. (1998). *Treating the tough adolescent.* New York: Guilford Press.

85 Barber, B. K. (Ed.). (2002). *Intrusive parenting: How psychological control affects children and adolescents.* Washington, DC: American Psychological Association.

86 Allport, G. (1958). *The nature of prejudice.* New York: Doubleday.

87 Garbarino, J., & de Lara, E. (2002). *And words can hurt forever: How to protect adolescents from bullying, harassment, and emotional violence.* New York: Free Press.

88 Wachtel, T. (2003). Restorative justice in everyday life: Beyond the formal ritual. *Reclaiming Children and Youth, 12*(2),83-87.

89 Shores, R., & Wehby, J. (1999). Analyzing the classroom social behavior of students with EBD. *Journal of Behavioral Disorders, 7*(4), 194-199.

90 Amini, F., Lannon, R., & Lewis, T. (2001). *A general theory of love.* New York: Vintage.

91 Reivich, K., & Shatte, A. (2002). *The resilience factor: Seven essential skills for overcoming life's inevitable obstacles.* New York: Broadway Books.

92 Knitzer, J., Steinberg, Z., & Fleisch, B. (1990). *At the schoolhouse door: An examination of programs and policies for children with behavioral and emotional problems.* New York: Bankstreet College of Education.

93 Csikszentmihalyi, M. (1996). *Creativity: Flow and the psychology of discovery and invention.* New York: HarperCollins Publishers. Csikszentmihalyi labels the natural motivation to pursue goals and solve problems as "flow". It is the foundation of creativity and mastery.

94 In everyday terms, "frustration" is often used to describe any unpleasant emotional state. Here we use the classical definition of Dollard and colleagues: the negative reaction resulting when goal-directed activity is obstructed. Dollard, J., Doob, L., Miller, N., Mowrer, O., & Sears, R. (1939). *Frustration and aggression.* New Haven: Yale University Press.

95 Redl, F. (1957). *When we deal with children.* Glencoe, IL: Free Press.

96 Undated personal communication from Mike Baizerman, University of Minnesota.

97 Wasmund, W., & Tate, T. (1996). *Partners in empowerment: A peer group primer.* Albion, MI: Starr Commonwealth.

98 Gold, M. (1995). Charting a course: Promise and prospects for alternative schools. *Journal of Emotional and Behavioral Problems, 3*(4), 8-11, Also, see: Gold, M., & Osgood, D. W. (1984), *Expelled to friendlier places.* Ann Arbor: University of Michigan Press.

99 Gold, M. & Osgood, D. W. (1992). *Personality and peer influence in juvenile corrections.* Westport, CT: Greenwood Press.

100 Higgins, G. (1994). *Resilient adults: Overcoming a cruel past.* San Francisco: Jossey-Bass, pp. 324-325.

101 Solnick, J., Braukmann, C., Bedlington, M., Kirigin, K., & Wolf, M. (1981). The relationship between parent-youth interaction and delinquency in group homes. *Journal of Abnormal Child Psychology, 9*(1), 107-119.

102 Long, N. J. (1997). The therapeutic power of kindness. *Reclaiming Children and Youth, 5*(4), 242-246.

103 Roddick, A. (ed.) (2003). *A revolution in kindness.* West Sussex, UK: Anita Roddick Books.

104 Tutu, D. (1997). Cited by M, Battle, *Reconciliation: The ubuntu theology of Desmond Tutu.* Cleveland, OH: Pilgrim Press, p. 27.

105 Montgomery, M. (1997). The powerlessness of punishment: Angry pride and delinquent identity. *Reclaiming Children and Youth, 6*(5), 162-166.

106 Rotherem-Borus, M. J., & Duan, N. (2003). Next generation of preventive interventions. *Child and Adolescent Psychiatry, 42*(5), 518-526.

107 Dodge, K., & Somberg, D. (1987). Hostile attribution biases among aggressive boys are exacerbated under conditions of threat to the self. *Child Development, 58,* 213-234.

108 Beck, A. (1999). *Prisoners of hate: The cognitive basis of anger, hostility, and violence*. New York, HarperCollins.

109 Fulcher, L. (2001). Cultural safety: Lessons from Maori wisdom, *Reclaiming Children and Youth, 10*(3), 153-157.

110 The issue of race is ignored in most conflict management models says James Cunningham. See: Cunningham, J. (2003). A "cool pose": Cultural perspectives on conflict management. *Reclaiming Children and Youth, 12*(2), 88-92. For training programs to address problems of racism, see: Newkirk, R. & Rutstein, N. (2000). *Racial healing*. Albion, MI: National Resource Center for the Healing of Racism.

111 Niehoff, D. (1999). *The biology of violence*. New York: Free Press.

112 Lewin, K., Lippit, R. & White, R. K. (1939). Patterns of aggressive behavior: An experimentally created "social climate." *Journal of Social Psychology, X*, 271-279,

113 Bell, D. M. & Ainsworth, M. (1972). Infant crying and maternal responsive lens. *Child Development, 43*, 1171-1190.

114 Patterson, G. R. (2002b). The early development of coercive family processes. In J. B. Reid, G. Patterson, & J. Snyder (Eds.), *Antisocial behavior in children and adolescents* (pp. 25-44). Washington, DC: American Psychological Association.

115 Travis Hirschi is the leading theorist on the relationship between social bonding and social control. See: Akers, R., & Sellers, C. (2004). *Criminological theories: introduction, evaluation, and application*. Los Angeles, CA: Roxbury Publishers.

116 Brendtro, L. Ness, A. & Mitchell, M. (2004). *No disposable kids*. Bloomington, IN: National Educational Service.

117 Jenkins, R. L. & Brown, W. (1988). *The abandonment of delinquent behavior*. New York: Praeger.

118 Patterson, G. R., Reid, I. & Eddy, M. (2002). A brief history of the Oregon model. In J. B. Reid, G. Patterson, & J. Snyder (Eds.), *Antisocial behavior in children and adolescents* (pp. 3-21), Washington, DC: American Psychological Association.

Chapter 3

119 Ramphele, M. (2002). *Steering by the stars: Being young in South Africa*. Cape Town: Tafelberg Publishers, p. 123.

120 Montaigne, M. (1580). On the education of children. In E. Trechman (Ed.), *The essays of Montaigne* (Vol. 1 & 2), (1927). Milford, UK: Oxford University Press.

121 Brendtro, L., & Ness, A. (1983). *Re-educating troubled youth.* New York: Aldine.

122 Brendtro, L., & Hinders, D. (1990). A saga of Janusz Korczak, the king of children. *Harvard Educational Review, 60*(2), 237-246.

123 Korczak, J. (1929). *When I am young again and The childs right to respect.* Translated by E. P. Kulawic. (1992). Lanham, MD: University Press of America, p. 468.

124 Bockhoven, J. S. (1956). Moral treatment in American psychiatry. *Journal of Mental and Nervous Diseases, 124*(3), 292-321.

125 Menninger, K. (1959). Hope, *American Journal of Psychiatry, 116,* 481-491.

126 Kilpatrick, W. H. (1928). *Education for a changing civilization.* New York: McMillan Company.

127 Wilker, K. (1920). *Der Lindenhof.* Translated 1993 by Stephan Lhotzky. Sioux Falls, SD: Augustana College, p, 69.

128 Paton, A. (1986). *Diepkloof: Reflections of Diepkloof reformatory.* Cape Town, South Africa: Credo Press.

129 Aspinwall, L. G., & Staudinger, U. M. (Eds.). (2003). *A psychology of human strengths.* Washington, DC: American Psychological Association.

130 Rogers, C. (1939). *The clinical treatment of the problem child.* Boston: Houghton Mifflin.

131 Freud, A. (1951). An experiment in group upbringing. In A, Freud, (1968), *The writings of Anna Freud (Vol. IV): Indications for child analysis and other papers,* p. 163-229. New York, International Universities Press.

132 Redl, F. (1957). *When we deal with children.* Glencoe, IL: Free Press.

133 White, M. (1995). *Reauthoring lives.* Adelaide, Australia: Dulwich Centre Publications, p. 5.

134 Menninger, K. (1963). *The vital balance.* New York: The Viking Press.

135 James, W. (1963). Cited in K. Menninger, *The vital balance.* New York: The Viking Press, p. 412.

136 Seligman, M., & Peterson, C. (2003). Positive clinical psychology. In L. G. Aspinwall & U, M. Staudinger (Eds.), *A psychology of human strengths* (pp. 305-318). Washington, DC: American Psychological Association, p. 314.

137 Levy, Z. (1993). *Negotiating positive identity in a group care community: Reclaiming uprooted youth.* New York: Haworth Press, p. 22.

138 Werner, E. (1995). Resilience and development. *American Psychological Society, 4,* 81-85.

139 Walsh, F. (1998). *Strengthening family resilience.* New York: Guilford Press.

140 Flach, F, (1989). *Resilience: Discovering a new strength at times of stress.* New York: Fawcett Columbine.

141 Werner, E., & Smith, R. (1992). *Overcoming the odds: high risk children from birth to adulthood.* Ithaca, NY: Cornell University Press.

142 O'Connor, T. G., Rutter, M., & English and Romanian Adoptees Study Team. (2000). Attachment disorder behavior following early severe deprivation: Extension and longitudinal follow-up. *Child and Adolescent Psychiatry, 39*(6), 703-712.

143 Werner, E. & Smith, R. (1992). *Overcoming the odds: high risk children from birth to adulthood.* Ithaca, NY: Cornell University Press.

144 Over a period of forty years, Michael Rutter and colleagues have conducted a host of longitudinal studies of children at risk, following them into adulthood. For a discussion of his key findings, see: Rutter, M. (1987). Psychosocial resilience and protective mechanisms. *American Journal of Orthopsychiatry, 57,* 316-331.

145 Garmezy, N. (1983). Stressors of childhood. In M. Rutter & N. Garmezy (Eds.), *Stress, coping and development in children* (pp. 43-84). New York: McGraw-Hill, p. 73.

146 The most widely used system for labeling mental health problems is the Diagnostic and Statistical Manual of Mental Disorders [DSM] published by the American Psychiatric Association, For a critique of the DSM approach, see: Buetler, M., & Malik, M. (Eds.). (2002). *Rethinking DSM* Washington, DC: American Psychological Association.

147 McClellan, J. M., & Werry, J. S. (2004). Evidence-based treatments in child and adolescent psychiatry: An inventory. *Child and Adolescent Psychiatry, 42*(12), 1388-1400.

148 McClellan, J. M., & Werry, J. S. (2000). Introduction: Research on psychiatric diagnostic interviews for children and adolescents. *Child and Adolescent Psychiatry, 39*(1), 19-27.

149 Seligman, M., & Peterson, C. (2003). Positive clinical psychology. In L. G. Aspinwall & U. M. Staudinger (Eds.), *A psychology of human strengths* (pp. 305-318). Washington, DC: American Psychological Association.

150 Scales, P. C., Benson, P. L., & Roehlkepartain, E. C. (2001). *Grading grown-ups: American adults report on their real relationships with kids.* Minneapolis, MN: Lutheran Brotherhood and Search Institute.

151 Tutu, D. (2002). Our hope for the future. In L. Brendtro, M. Brokenleg, & S. Van Bockern, *Reclaiming youth at risk* (Rev. ed.). Bloomington, IN: National Educational Service, p. x.

152 Toobey, J., & Cosmides, L. (1990). On the universality of human nature and the uniqueness of the individual. The role of genetics and adaptation. *Journal of Personality, 58,* 17-68.

153 Toobey, J., & Cosmides, L. (1992). Psychological foundations of culture. In J. Barkow, L. Cosmides, & J. Toobey (Eds.), *The adaptive mind* (pp. 19-136). New York: Oxford University Press.

154 Brendtro, L., & Shahbazian, M. (2004). *Troubled children and youth: Turning problems into opportunity.* Champaign, IL: Research Press.

155 Coopersmith, S. (1967). *The antecedents of self-esteem.* San Francisco: W. H. Freeman.

156 Benard, B. (2004). *Resiliency: What we have learned.* San Francisco: WestEd.

157 This discussion draws from evaluation data on 2,652 youth from the Search Institute prepared by Wendy L. Tackett for the Coordinating Council of Calhoun County Michigan, Battle Creek, 2004.

158 Benson, P. (1997). *All kids are our kids: What communities must do to raise caring and responsible children and adolescents.* San Francisco: Jossey-Bass.

159 Baumeister, R. F., & Leary, M, R. (1995). The need to belong: Desire for interpersonal attachments as a fundamental human motivation. *Psychological Bulletin, 117,* 479-529.

160 Cassidy, J., & Shaver, P. (1999). *Handbook of attachment: Theory, research and clinical applications.* New York: Guilford Press.

161 Johnson, S. (2003). Emotions and the brain. *Discover, 24*(4), 62-69.

162 Provine, R. (2000). *Laughter: A scientific investigation.* New York: The Viking Press.

163 Proverbs 17:22, *Holy Bible* (Revised Standard Version).

164 Harlow, H. F. (1958). The nature of love. *American Psychologist, 13,*673-685.

165 White, R. (1959). Motivation reconsidered: The concept of competence. *Psychological Review, 66,* 297-313.

166 Csikszentmihalyi, M., Rathunde, K., & Whalen, S. (1993). *Talented teenagers.* Melbourne, Australia: Cambridge University Press.

167 The phrase "Just Manageable Difficulties" is a restatement of Vygotsky's (1989) "zone of proximal development" by Nicholas Hobbs. See: Hobbs, N. (1994). *The troubled and troubling child.* Cleveland: AREA. This is the level of challenge beyond current independent problem solving, which uses the added skills of adult guidance or more skillful peers. When youth are working with Just Manageable Difficulties, the problem-solving brain is at its best. Brain scans show that active areas of the brain burn glucose (blood sugar), the body's major source of energy. The problem-solving brain burns lots of calories when attending to a new and challenging task. It shuts down if the task is too boring or too difficult. And, if some event is highly threatening, the thinking areas go dark as energy is diverted to the emotional and reptilian brain areas that prepare for fight or flight.

168 Dewey, J. (1910). *How we think.* Lexington, MA: D. C, Heath.

169 Sternberg, R. J. (1997). *Successful intelligence.* New York: Plume Books.

170 Sternberg, R. J. (2000). The concept of intelligence, In R. J. Sternberg (Ed.), *The handbook of intelligence* (pp. 3-15). Cambridge, MA: Yale University Press.

171 Mayer, J., Salovey, P., & Caruso, D. (2000). Models of emotional intelligence. In R. J. Sternberg (Ed.), *The handbook of intelligence* (pp. 396-422). Cambridge, MA: Yale University Press.

172 Greenspan, S. I. (1997). *The growth of the mind*. Cambridge, MA: Perseus, p. 213.

173 Bandura, A. (1995). Exercise of personal and collective efficacy in changing societies. In A. Bandura (Ed.), *Self-efficacy and changing societies* (pp. 1-45). New York: Cambridge University Press.

174 Ford, D. H. (1994). *Humans as self-constructing, living systems: A developmental perspective on behavior and personality*. State College, PA: Ideals, Inc.

175 Rutter, J. B. (1954). *Social learning and clinical psychology*. Englewood Cliffs, NJ: Prentice Hall.

176 Desetta, A., & Wolin, S. (2000). *The struggle to be strong*. Minneapolis, MN: Free Spirit.

177 Long, N., Wood, M, & Fecser, F. (2001). *Life space crisis intervention*. Austin, TX: PRO-ED.

178 Cobb, S. (1976). Social support as a moderator of life stress. *Psychosomatic Medicine, 38*, 300-314.

179 Hoffman, M. L. (1981). Is altruism part of human nature? *Journal of Personality and Social Psychology, 40,* 120-137.

180 Gibbs, J. C. (1994). Fairness and empathy as the foundation for universal moral education. *Comenius, 14*, 12-23.

181 Greenspan, S. I. (1995). *The challenging child*. Reading, MA: AddisonWesley.

182 Odney, J., & Brendtro, L. (1992). Students grade their schools. *Journal of Emotional and Behavioral Problems, 2*(1), 4-9. p. 8.

183 Buber, M. (1970). *I and thou*. New York: Charles Scribner and Sons.

184 Coles, R. (1990). *The spiritual life of children*. Boston: Houghton-Mifflin.

185 Larson, S., & Brendtro, L, (2000). *Reclaiming our prodigal sons and daughters*. Bloomington, IN: National Educational Service.

186 Ali, M., & Ali, L. (2004). Foreword in L. Brendtro, A. Ness, & M. Mitchell, *No disposable kids*. Bloomington, IN: National Educational Service, p. x.

Chapter 4

187 Gannon, B. (2003). The improbable relationship. *Relational Child and Youth Care, 16*(3),6-9, p, 8.

188 Bronfenbrenner, U. (1986). Alienation and the four worlds of childhood, *Phi Delta Kappan, 67*, 430-436.

189 Palmer, P. (1998). *The courage to teach.* San Francisco: Jossey-Bass, p. 40.

190 Hallowell, E. (2002). Connections. National Adolescent Conference, Scottsdale, Arizona, May 31, 2002. Ben Franklin Institute.

191 Hall, S. (1829). *Lectures on school-keeping.* Boston: Richardson, Lord, and Holbrook, p. 47.

192 Pfister, O. (1956). Therapy and ethics in August Aichhorn's treatment of wayward youth. In K. R. Eisler (Ed.), *Searchlights on delinquency* (pp. 35-49). New York: International Universities Press, p. 40.

193 Seita, J. & Brendtro, L. (2004). *Kids who outwit adults.* Bloomington, IN: National Educational Service.

194 Montague, A., & Matson, F. (1979). *The human connection.* New York: McGraw-Hill.

195 Garfat, T. (1995). *The effective child and youth care intervention: A phenomenological inquiry.* Doctoral dissertation. Victoria, BC: University of Victoria.

196 Krueger, M. (1998). *Youth work resources.* Washington, DC: CWLA Press.

197 This involves the amygdala in humans as in other mammals. Connections can even be made across species because of the mutual interest certain "tame" mammals have in one another. Thus pets can become very loyal and serve as substitutes for supportive human connections.

198 Burgoon, J., Buller, D., & Woodall, W. (1996). Nonverbal communication: *The unspoken dialogue.* New York: McGraw-Hill.

199 Maier, H. (1987). *Developmental group care of children.* New York: Haworth Press.

200 Krueger, M. (1998). *Youth work resources.* Washington, DC: CWLA Press.

201 Hubble, M., Duncan, B., & Miller, S. (1999). *The heart and soul of change: What works in therapy.* Washington, DC: American Psychological Association.

202 Seligman, M. (1975). *Helplessness: On depression, development, and death.* San Francisco: W. H. Freeman.

203 Bowlby, J. (1988). *A secure base: Parent, child attachments and healthy human development.* New York: Basic Books. The need for attachment transcends all cultures. Ainsworth, M. (1967). *Infancy in Uganda.* Baltimore: Johns Hopkins University Press.

204 Garbarino, J., & de Lara, E. (2002). *And words can hurt forever: How to protect adolescents from bullying, harassment, and emotional violence.* New York: Free Press.

205 Gottman, J. (2001). *The relationship cure.* New York: Three Rivers Press.

206 Scheff, T. (1995). Self-defense against verbal assault: Shame, anger, and the social bond. *Family Process, 34,* 271-286.

207 Vygotsky, L. S. (1989). *Thought and language.* Cambridge, MA: MIT Press.

208 Larson, S., & Brendtro, L. (2000). *Reclaiming our prodigal sons and daughters.* Bloomington, IN: National Educational Services.

209 Duncan, B. L., Hubble, M.A., & Miller, S.D, (1997). *Psychotherapy with "impossible" cases.* New York: Norton.

210 Anglin, J. (2003). *Pain, normality, and the struggle for congruence: Reinterpreting residential care for children and youth.* Binghamton, NY: Haworth Press.

211 de Becker, G. (1998). *The gift of fear.* New York: Dell.

212 Long, N. J., & Dufner, B. (1980). The stress cycle or the coping cycle: The impact of home and school stresses on pupil's classroom behavior. In N. J. Long, W. C, Morse, & R. G. Newman (Eds.), *Conflict in the classroom* (4th ed.) (pp. 218-228). Belmont, CA: Wadsworth Publishing Company.

213 Lynch, J. J. (1977). *The broken heart: The medical consequences of loneliness.* New York: Basic Books.

214 Kowalsky, R. M. (1999). Speaking the unspeakable: Self-disclosure and mental health. In R. M. Kowalsky & M. R. Leary (Eds.), *The social psychology of emotional and behavior problems* (pp. 225-248). Washington, DC: American Psychological Association.

215 Thompson, G. & Jenkins, J. (1993). *Verbal judo: The gentle art of persuasion.* New York: William Morrow.

216 Thompson, G., & Jenkins, J. (1993). *Verbal judo: The gentle art of persuasion.* New York: William Morrow, p. 67.

217 Freud, S. (1997). Cited in S. D. Miller, B. L. Duncan, & M.A. Hubble, *Escape from Babel: Toward a unifying language for psychotherapy practice.* New York: W,W. Norton, p. 60.

218 Scheff, T. (1995). Self-defense against verbal assault: Shame, anger, and the social bond. *Family Process, 34,* 271-286.

219 Kozart, M. (2002). Understanding efficacy and psychotherapy: An ethnomethodological perspective on the therapeutic alliance. *American Journal of Orthopsychiatry, 72*(2), 217-231.

220 Key, E. (1900). *Barnets Århundrade* [The Century of the Child]. English edition published in 1909. New York: G. P. Putnam.

221 Diel, P. (1987). *The psychology of reeducation*. Translated by Raymond Rosenthal. Boston: Chambhala.

222 Gottman, J. (2001). The relationship cure. New York: Three Rivers Press; Patterson, G. R (2002). The early development of coercive family processes. In J. B. Reid, G. Patterson, & J. Snyder (Eds.), *Antisocial behavior in children and adolescents* (pp. 25-44). Washington, DC: American Psychological Association.

223 Blanchard, G. (1995). *The difficult connection*. Brandon, VT: Safer Society Press.

224 Willner, A., Braukmann, C., Kirigin, K., Fixsen, D., Phillips, E. & Wolf, M. (1970). The training and validation of youth-preferred social behaviors of child-care personnel. *Journal of Applied Behavior Analysis, 10*(2), 219-230.

225 Artz, S., Nicholson, D., Halsall, E., & Larke, S. (2001). *Guide for needs assessment for youth*. Victoria, BC: University of Victoria School of Child and Youth Care.

Chapter 5

226 Angelou, M. (2002). Cited in M. Ramphele, *Steering by the stars: Being young in South Africa*. Cape Town: Tafelberg Publishers, p. 17.

227 Toch, H., & Adams, K. (2002). *Acting out*. Washington, DC: American Psyhological Association.

228 Formal training in the skills of this model is provided by non-profit organizations associated with the Reclaiming Youth Network. See: http://www.reclaiming.com

229 Wallin, B. (1994). *Giving the boot to boot camps*, Master's Thesis, Augustana College, Sioux Falls, SD; Hewitt, J. P. (1998). *The myth of self esteem*. New York: St. Martin's; Goldstein, A. P. & Martens, B. K. (2000). *Lasting change: Methods for enhancing generalization of gain*. Champaign, IL: Research Press.

230 Dishion, T. J., & Kavanagh, K. (2003). *Intervening in adolescent problem behavior: A family-centered approach*. New York: The Guilford Press.

231 Mathur, S. R. & Rutherford, R B. (1996). Is social skills training effective for students with emotional and behavioral disorders? Research issues and needs. *Behavioral Disorders, 22*, 21-28.

232 Detterman, D. K. (1993). The case for the prosecution transfer as an epiphenomenon. In D. K. Detterman & R. J. Sternberg (Eds.), *Transfer on trial, intelligence cognition, and instruction* (pp. 1-24). Norwood, NJ: Ablex.

233 Goldstein, A. P., & Martens, B. K. (2000). *Lasting change: Methods for enhancing generalization of gain.* Champaign, IL: Research Press.

234 Dewey, J. (1910). *How we think.* Lexington, MA: D. C. Heath, p. 72.

235 Mechanic, D. (1978). *Students under stress: A study in the social psychology of adaptation.* Madison, WI: The University of Wisconsin Press.

236 Lazarus, R. & Folkman, S. (1984). *Stress, appraisal, and coping.* New York: Springer.

237 Murphy, L. B., & Moriarty, A. E. (1976). *Vulnerability, coping, and growth: From infancy to adolescence.* New Haven, CT: Yale University Press.

238 Murphy, L. B., & Moriarty, A. E. (1976). *Vulnerability, coping, and growth: From infancy to adolescence.* New Haven, CT: Yale University Press.

239 Murphy, L. B., & Moriarty, A. E. (1976). *Vulnerability, coping, and growth: From infancy to adolescence.* New Haven, CT: Yale University Press, p. 263.

240 Mowrer, O. H. (1947). On the dual nature of learning: A reinterpretation of "conditioning" and "problem-solving". *Harvard Educational Review, 17,* 102-148.

241 Piaget, J. (1952). *The origins of intelligence in children.* New York: W. W. Norton.

242 The Zeigarnik effect is named after Russian psychologist Bluma Zeigarnik who first discovered this phenomenon. Zeigarnik, B. (1927). Das Behalten von erledigten und unerledigten Handlungen (The memory of completed and uncompleted tasks). *Psychologische Forschung, 9,* 1-85.

243 Lewin, K. (1935). *A dynamic theory of personality. Selected papers.* New York: McGraw; Zeigarnik, B. (1927). Das Behalten von erledigten und unerledigten Handlungen (The memory of completed and uncompleted tasks). *Psychologische Forschung, 9,* 1-85.

244 Ford, D. H. (1994). *Humans as self-constructing living systems.* State College, PA: Ideals.

245 Fromm, E. (1998). Lost and found a half century later. Letters by Freud and Einstein. *American Psychologist 53*(10), 1195-1198.

246 Meichenbaum, D., & Fong, G. T. (1993). Toward a theoretical model of the role of reasons in non-adherence to health-related advice. In D. M. Wegner & J. W. Pennebaker (Eds.), *Handbook of mental control* (pp. 473-490). Englewood Cliffs, NJ: Prentice-Hall.

247 Redl worked with Anna Freud and August Aichhorn in a residential school in Austria. See: Aichhorn, A. (1935). *Wayward youth*. New York: Viking Press. Viewed in terms of the RAP approach discussed in these chapters, Aichhorn was a master at *connecting* with distrustful kids. He helped kids clarify challenging life events, such as a theft or truancy. And, he rejected coercive methods but worked to *restore* broken relationships.

248 Redl piloted small residential treatment groups with aggressive children in Michigan and in an experimental program at the National Institute for Mental Health with Nicholas Long in Washington, DC. He collaborated with David Wineman and William Morse at the University of Michigan Fresh Air Camp where generations of graduate students received front-line training in therapeutic work with troubled children. This led to two classic books by Redl and Wineman, *Children Who Hate* (1951) and *Controls from Within* (1952). These books were later consolidated in the volume *The Aggressive Child* (Redl & Wineman, 1957.) Subsequent works extending that approach include: *The Other 23 Hours* (Trieschman, Whittaker, & Brendtro, 1969); *Re-Educating Troubled Youth* (Brendtro & Ness, 1983), *The Education and Treatment of Socioemotionally Impaired Children* (Morse, 1985), and *Conflict in the Classroom* (Long, Morse, & Newman, 1997).

249 Redl's use of stories of events was an early application of what is now well known as the narrative therapy movement, such as advocated by Michael White of Australia and David Epston of New Zealand. See: White, M., & Epston, D. (1990). *Narrative means to therapeutic ends*. New York: W. W. Norton.

250 Redl, F. (1994). The oppositional child and the confronting adult: A mind to mind encounter. In E. James Anthony & Doris G. Gilpin (Eds.), *The clinical faces of childhood* (Vol. 1) (pp. 41-57), Northvale, NJ: Jason Aronson, Inc., p. 53.

251 Baker, S., & Gersten, R. (2000). *Balancing qualitative/quantitative research.* Paper presented to OSEP Research Project Director's Conference, Washington, DC, July 14, 2000.

252 Csikszentmihalyi, M. (1990). *Flow: The psychology of optimal experience.* New York: Harper Perennial.

253 Gibbs, J. C. (1979). The meaning of ecologically oriented inquiry in contemporary psychology. *American Psychologist, 34,* 127-140.

254 Forgus, R. H. & Shulman, B. H. (1979). *Personality: A cognitive view.* Englewood Cliffs, NJ: Prentice-Hall.

255 Ford, D. H. (1994). *Humans as self-constructing living systems.* State College, PA: Ideals.

256 Yalom, I. (1995). *The theory and practice of group psychotherapy* (4th ed.). New York: Basic Books.

257 Bruner, J. (1990). *Acts of meaning*. Cambridge, MA: Harvard University Press; Sternberg, R. J. (2000). The concept of intelligence. In R. J. Sternberg (Ed.), *The handbook of intelligence* (pp. 3-15). Cambridge, MA: Yale University Press.

258 Pennebaker, J. (1990). *Opening up*. New York: Morrow.

259 White, M. (1995). *Re-authoring lives*. Adelaide, Australia: Dulwich Centre Publications.

260 Bruner, J. (1990). *Acts of meaning*. Cambridge, MA: Harvard University Press.

261 Miller, W., & Rollnick, S. (1991). *Preparing people to change addictive behavior*. New York: Guilford Press.

262 Dishion, T. J. & Kavanagh, K. (2003). *Intervening in adolescent problem behavior: A family-centered approach*. New York: The Guilford Press.

263 Adapted from Peterson, J. S. (2003). Listening: Resisting the urge to fix them. In K. McCluskey & A. Mays, *Mentoring for talent development* (pp. 126-142). Sioux Falls, SD: Reclaiming Youth International.

264 We credit this concept to Mark Freado of the American Re-Education Association.

265 Long, N, J., & Dufner, B. (1980). The stress cycle or the coping cycle: The impact of home and school stresses on pupil's classroom behavior. In Nicholas J. Long, William C. Morse, & Ruth G. Newman (Eds.), *Conflict in the classroom* (4th ed.) (pp. 218-228). Belmont, CA: Wadsworth Publishing Company.

266 Flach, F. (1989). *Resilience: Discovering a new strength at times of stress*. New York: Fawcett Columbine.

267 Scheff, T. (1995). Self-defense against verbal assault: Shame, anger, and the social bond. *Family Process, 34*, 271-286.

268 Toch, H., & Adams, K. (2002). *Acting out*. Washington, DC: American Psychological Association.

269 Patterson, G. R. (2002a). Future extensions of the models. In J. Reid, G. Patterson, & J. Snyder (Eds.) *Antisocial behavior in children and adolescents* (pp. 273-283). Washington, DC: American Psychological Association.

270 Zillmann, D. (1993). Mental control of angry aggression. In D. Wegner & J. Pennebaker (Eds.) *Handbook of mental control* (pp. 370-392). Upper Saddle River, NJ: Prentice-Hall.

271 Gibbs, J., Potter, G. & Goldstein, A.(1995) *The EQUIP program: Teaching youth to think and act responsibly through a peer-helping approach*. Champaign, IL: Research Press.

272 Le Doux, J., & Phelps, E. (2000). Emotional networks in the brain. In M. Lewis, & J. M. Haviland-Jones (Eds.), *Handbook of Emotions* (2nd ed.) (pp. 157-172). New York: Guilford.

273 Greenspan, S. I. (1997). *The growth of the mind and the endangered origins of intelligence.* Cambridge, MA: Perseus Books.

274 Clarke, J. I. (1999). *Connections: The threads that strengthen families.* Center City, MN: Hazelden.

275 Zillmann, D. (1993). Mental control of angry aggression. In D. Wegner & J, Pennebaker (Eds,), *Handbook of mental control* (pp. 370-392). Upper Saddle River, NJ: Prentice-Hall.

276 Clarke, J. I. (1999). *Connections: The threads that strengthen families.* Center City, MN: Hazelden.

277 Toch, H., & Adams, K. (2002). *Acting out.* Washington, DC: American Psychological Association.

278 Murphy, L. B., & Moriarty, A. E. (1976). *Vulnerability, coping, and growth: From infancy to adolescence.* New Haven, CT: Yale University Press.

279 Vorrath, H. & Brendtro, L. (1985). Positive peer culture. The authors report for studies of significant achievement gains in achievement schools for learners at risk who initially were achieving significantly below norms. After creating a climate of respectful relationships, the average achievement of all students in these schools rose to 1.5 grade levels per year in the program.

280 A common question is how RAP relates to other "here and now" therapeutic models such as Reality Therapy, Life Space Crisis Intervention, Positive Peer Culture, and Solution-Focused Therapy. These more formal models require advanced levels of training in sophisticated therapeutic techniques and are usually designed for specific problems and populations. RAP builds on existing strengths and natural helping processes to foster climates with respectful relationships and responsible behaviour. Thus, it complements other strength-based therapy approaches. It is also a useful enrichment to crisis intervention models since it builds climates that prevent violence and abuse.
RAP training is based on universal design so it can be delivered across varied ages, educational levels, work roles, and settings. RAP allows common training of staff, young persons, parents, and volunteers so that there is a unifying theme in a setting or community. RAP interventions are efficient and can be adjusted to whatever time is available, whether momentary encounters or extended relationships. RAP is grounded in cross-cultural studies of resilience and brain research so it applies across varied cultural backgrounds. RAP principles are multi-modal and evidence-based, supported by a wide range of research as seen in the accompanying bibliography. RAP principles are also value-based and consistent with statements of the rights of children. The reclaiming and restorative philosophy is also consonant with spiritual traditions that call for treating all persons with dignity and fostering the oneness of humankind

281 Seita, J., Mitchell, M., & Tobin, C. (1996). *In whose best interest? One child's odyssey, a nation's responsibility.* Elizabethtown, PA: Continental Press.

282 Gladwell, M. (2002). *The tipping point: How little things can make a big difference.* New York: Little, Brown and Company.

283 Miller, W. & Rollnick, S. (1991). *Preparing people to change addictive behavior.* New York: Guilford Press.

284 Excerpts from: Lay, J. (2000). The person behind the file number. *Reclaiming Children and Youth, 9*(2), 68-69.

Chapter 6

285 Mandela, N. (2003). A fabric of care. In K. Asmal, D. Chidester, & W. James (Eds.), *Nelson Mandela: From freedom to the future* (pp. 416-418). Johannesburg: Jonathan Ball Publishers, p. 418.

286 Mandela, N. (2003). A society's soul. In K. Asmal, D. Chidester, & W. James (Eds.), *Nelson Mandela: From freedom to the future* (pp. 421-423). Johannesburg: Jonathan Ball Publishers, p, 421.

287 Gibbs, J. C. (1994). Fairness and empathy as the foundation for universal moral education. *Comenius, 14,* 12-23.

288 Tutu, D. (1997). Cited in M. Battle, *Reconciliation: The ubuntu theology of Desmond Tutu.* Cleveland, OH: Pilgrim Press.

289 Hadley, M. (Ed.). (2001). *The spiritual roots of restorative justice.* Albany, NY: State University of New York Press.

290 Zehr, H. (2002). *The little book of restorative justice.* Intercourse, PA: Good Books.

291 Portions of this chapter are adapted from: Gibbs, J., Potter, G., Goldstein, A. & Brendtro, L. (1996). From harassment to helping with antisocial youth: The EQUIP program, *Reclaiming Children and Youth, 5*(1), 40-46.

292 Gold, M., & Osgood, D. W. (1992). *Personality and peer influence in juvenile corrections.* Westport, CT: Greenwood Press.

293 Goldstein, A. P. (1993). Interpersonal skills training intervention. In A.P. Goldstein & C. R. Huff (Eds.), *The gang intervention handbook* (pp. 87-157). Champaign, IL: Research Press.

294 Dishion, T., French, D., and Patterson, G. (1995). The development and ecology of anti-social behavior. In D. Cicchetti & D. J. Cohen (Eds.), *Developmental psychopathology: Vol. 2: Risk, disorder, and adaptation.* (pp. 421-471). New York: Wiley.

295 Dishion, T., McCord, J., & Poulin, F. (1999). When interventions harm: Peer groups and problem behavior. *American Psychologist, 54*(9), pp. 755-764.

Bibliography

Adler, A. (1930). *Die seele des schwererzeihbaren schulkindes*. Translated into English in 1963, *The Problem Child*. New York: G. P. Putnam's Sons.

Adler, M. (1985). *Ten philosophical mistakes*. New York: Macmillan.

Aggleton, J. P. (Ed.). (2000). *The amygdala: A functional analysis*. Oxford, UK: Oxford University Press.

Aichhorn, A. (1938). *Wayward youth*. New York: Viking Press.

Akers, R., & Sellers, C. (2004). *Criminological theories: Introduction, evaluation, and application*. Los Angeles: Roxbury Publishers.

Allport, G. (1958). *The nature of prejudice*. New York: Doubleday.

Ali, M., & Ali, L. (2004). Foreword in L. Brendtro, A. Ness, & M. Mitchell, *No disposable kids*. Bloomington, IN: National Educational Service.

Amini, F., Lannon, R., & Lewis, T. (2001). *A general theory of love*. New York: Vintage.

Angelou, M. (2002). Cited in M. Ramphele, *Steering by the stars: Being young in South Africa*. Cape Town: Tafelberg Publishers.

Anglin, J. (2003). *Pain, normality, and the struggle for congruence: Reinterpreting residential care for children and youth*. Binghamton, NY: Haworth Press.

Arnold, M. B. (1960). *Emotion and personality* (Vols. 1-2). New York: Columbia University Press.

Artz, S. (1998). *Sex, power, & the violent school girl*. New York: Columbia University Press.

Artz, S., Nicholson, D., Halsall, E., & Larke, S. (2001). *Guide for needs assessment for youth*. Victoria, BC: University of Victoria School of Child and Youth Care.

Asmal, K., Chidester, D., & James, W. (Eds.). *Nelson Mandela: From freedom to the future*. Johannesburg: Jonathan Ball Publishers

Aspinwall, L. G., & Staudinger, U. M. (Eds.). (2003). *A psychology of human strengths*. Washington, DC: American Psychological Association.

Baker, S., & Gersten, R. (2000). *Balancing qualitative/quantitative research.* Paper presented to OSEP Research Project Director's Conference, Washington, DC, July 14, 2000.

Bandura, A. (1995). Exercise of personal and collective efficacy in changing societies. In A. Bandura (Ed.), *Self-efficacy and changing societies* (pp. 1-45). New York: Cambridge University Press.

Barber, B. K. (Ed.). (2002). *Intrusive parenting: How psychological control affects children and adolescents.* Washington, DC: American Psychological Association.

Barnett, S., dos Reis, S., Riddle, M., & the Maryland Youth Practice Improvement Committee for Mental Health. (2002). Improving the management of acute aggression in state residential and inpatient psychiatric facilities for youths. *Child and Adolescent Psychiatry, 41*(8), 897-905.

Baumeister, R. F., & Leary, M. R. (1995). The need to belong: Desire for interpersonal attachments as a fundamental human motivation. *Psychological Bulletin, 117*: 479-529.

BBC. (1997). *Monty Roberts: A real horse whisperer.* (VHS). London: BBC Video.

Beck, A. (1999). *Prisoners of hate: The cognitive basis of anger, hostility, and violence.* New York: HarperCollins.

Bell, D. M., & Ainsworth, M. (1972). Infant crying and maternal responsive lens. *Child Development, 43,* 1171-1190.

Benard, B. (2004). *Resiliency: What we have learned.* San Francisco: WestEd.

Benson, E. (2003). Researchers are still looking for consensus on how and when anger first appears in infants. *Monitor on Psychology, 34*(3), 50-51.

Benson, P. (1997). *All kids are our kids: What communities must do to raise caring and responsible children and adolescents.* San Francisco: Jossey-Bass.

Bettelheim, B. (1974). *A home for the heart.* London: Thames and Hudson.

Blanchard, G. (1995). *The difficult connection.* Brandon, VT: Safer Society Press.

Bockhoven, J. S. (1956). Moral treatment in American psychiatry. *Journal of Mental and Nervous Diseases, 124*(3), 292-321.

Bowlby, J. (1988). *A secure base: Parent, child attachments and healthy human development.* New York: Basic Books. The need for attachment transcends all cultures. Ainsworth, M. (1967). *Infancy in Uganda.* Baltimore: Johns Hopkins University Press.

Brendtro, L. (2004). Rethinking coercive interventions with troubled youth: Harmonising values, research, and practice. A paper presented to the Alliance for Children and Families conference, Naples, Florida, January 16, 2004.

Brendtro, L., & Hinders, D. (1990). A saga of Janusz Korczak, the king of children. *Harvard Educational Review, 60*(2), 237-246.

Brendtro, L., & Ness, A. (1983). *Re-educating troubled youth.* New York: Aldine.

Brendtro, L., Brokenleg, M., & Van Bockern, S. (2002). *Reclaiming youth at risk: Our hope for the future* (Rev. ed.). Bloomington, IN: National Educational Service.

Brendtro, L., Ness, A., & Mitchell, M. (2004). *No disposable kids.* Bloomington, IN: National Educational Service.

Brendtro, L., & Shahbazian, M. (2004). *Troubled children and youth: Turning problems into opportunity.* Champaign, IL: Research Press.

Bronfenbrenner, U. (1986). Alienation and the four worlds of childhood. *Phi Delta Kappan, 67*, 430-436.

Bruner, J. (1990). *Acts of meaning.* Cambridge, MA: Harvard University Press.

Buber, M. (1970). *I and thou.* New York: Charles Scribner and Sons.

Buetler, M., & Malik, M. (Eds.). (2002). *Rethinking DSM.* Washington, DC: American Psychological Association.

Burgoon, J., Buller, D., & Woodall, W. (1996). *Nonverbal communication: The unspoken dialogue.* New York: McGraw-Hill.

Cassidy, J., & Shaver, P. (1999). *Handbook of attachment: Theory, research, and clinical applications.* New York: Guilford Press.

Centre, D. B., & Calloway, J. M. (1999). Self-reported job stress and personality in teachers of students with emotional or behavioural disorders. *Behavioural Disorders, 25*(1), 41-51.

Clarke, J. I. (1999). *Connections: The threads that strengthen families.* Centre City, MN: Hazelden.

Cobb, S. (1976). Social support as a moderator of life stress. *Psychosomatic Medicine, 38*, 300-314.

Coles, R. (1990). *The spiritual life of children*. Boston: Houghton-Mifflin.

Coopersmith, S. (1967). *The antecedents of self-esteem*. San Francisco: W. H. Freeman.

Courtenay, B. (1989). *The power of one*. Camberwell, Victoria, Australia: Penguin Books.

Crisis Prevention Institute. (2001). Protecting kids in restraint. *Reclaiming Children and Youth, 10*(2), 162-163.

Csikszentmihalyi, M. (1990). *Flow: The psychology of optimal experience.* New York: Harper Perennial.

Csikszentmihalyi, M. (1996). *Creativity: Flow and the psychology of discovery and invention.* New York: HarperCollins.

Csikszentmihalyi, M., Rathunde, K., & Whalen, S. (1993). *Talented teenagers.* Melbourne, Australia: Cambridge University Press.

Cunningham, J. (2003). A "cool pose": Cultural perspectives on conflict management. *Reclaiming Children and Youth, 12*(2), 88-92.

Davis, L. (1987). *Rivers of pain, bridges of hope.* Hong Kong: Writer's and Publisher's Cooperative.

de Becker, G. (1998). *The gift of fear.* New York: Dell.

de Mause, L. (1974). *The history of childhood.* New York: The Psychohistory Press.

Desetta, A., & Wolin, S. (2000). *The struggle to be strong.* Minneapolis, MN: Free Spirit.

Detterman, D. K. (1993). The case for the prosecution transfer as an epiphenomenon. In D. K. Detterman & R. J. Sternberg (Eds.), *Transfer on trial, intelligence cognition, and instruction* (pp. 1-24). Norwood, NJ: Ablex.

Dewey, J. (1910). *How we think.* Lexington, MA: D. C. Heath.

Diel, P. (1987). *The psychology of reeducation.* (Raymond Rosenthal, Trans.). Boston: Chambhala.

Dishion, T., French, D., & Patterson, G. R. (1995). The development and ecology of antisocial behaviour. In D. Chicchetti & D. J. Cohen (Eds.), *Developmental psychopathology: Volume 2: Risk, disorder, and adaptation* (pp. 421-471). New York: Wiley.

Dishion, T., & Kavanagh, K. (2002). The adolescent transitions program: A family-centred prevention strategy for schools. In J. Reid, G. Patterson, & J. Snyder, (Eds.), *Antisocial behaviour in children and adolescents* (pp. 257-272). Washington, DC: American Psychological Association.

Dishion, T. J., & Kavanagh, K. (2003). *Intervening in adolescent problem behaviour: A family-centred approach*. New York: The Guilford Press.

Dishion, T., McCord, J., & Poulin, F. (1999). When interventions harm: Peer groups and problem behaviour. *American Psychologist, 54*(9), 755-764.

Dodge, K., & Somberg, D. (1987). Hostile attribution biases among aggressive boys are exacerbated under conditions of threat to the self. *Child Development, 58,* 213-234.

Dollard, J., Doob, L., Miller, N., Mowrer, O., & Sears, R. (1939). *Frustration and aggression.* New Haven: Yale University Press.

Donovan, J., Jesser, R., & Costa, S. (1988). Syndrome of problem behaviour in adolescents. A replication. *Journal of Consulting and Clinical Psychology, 56*, 762-765.

Duncan, B. L., Hubble, M. A., & Miller, S. D. (1997). *Psychotherapy with "impossible" cases*. New York: Norton.

Durkheim, E. (1972). *Emile Durkheim: Selected writings*. Edited by Anthony Giddens. Cambridge, UK: Cambridge University Press.

Eisenberger, N., Lieberman, M., & Williams, K. (2003). The pain of social exclusion. *Science, 302*, 290-292.

Eisler, R. (1987). *The chalice and the blade: Our history, our future*. San Francisco: HarperCollins.

Empe, L., & Stafford, M. (1991). *American delinquency: Its meaning and construction.* Belmont, CA: Wadsworth Publishing Company.

Flach, F. (1989). *Resilience: Discovering a new strength at times of stress.* New York: Fawcett Columbine.

Ford, D. H. (1994). *Humans as self-constructing, living systems: A developmental perspective on behaviour and personality*. State College, PA: Ideals, Inc.

Forgus, R. H., & Shulman, B. H. (1979). *Personality: A cognitive view.* Englewood Cliffs, NJ: Prentice-Hall.

Freud, A. (1951). An experiment in group upbringing. In A. Freud, (1968), *The writings of Anna Freud (Vol. IV): Indications for child analysis and other papers* (pp. 163-229). New York: International Universities Press.

Freud, S. (1997). Cited in S. D. Miller, B. L. Duncan, & M. A. Hubble, *Escape from Babel: Toward a unifying language for psychotherapy practice.* New York: W.W. Norton.

Fromm, E. (1941). *Escape from freedom.* New York: Holt, Rinehart, and Winston.

Fromm, E. (1998). Lost and found a half century later. Letters by Freud and Einstein. *American Psychologist 53*(10), 1195-1198.

Fulcher, L. (2001). Cultural safety: Lessons from Maori wisdom. *Reclaiming Children and Youth, 10*(3), 153-157.

Gannon, B. (2003). The improbable relationship. *Relational Child and Youth Care, 16*(3), 6-9.

Garbarino, J. (1999). *Lost boys.* New York: Free Press.

Garbarino, J., & deLara, E. (2002). *And words can hurt forever: How to protect adolescents from bullying, harassment, and emotional violence.* New York: Free Press.

Garfat, T. (1995). *The effective child and youth care intervention: A phenomenological inquiry.* Doctoral dissertation. Victoria, BC: University of Victoria.

Garmezy, N. (1983). Stressors of childhood. In M. Rutter & N. Garmezy (Eds.), *Stress, coping and development in children* (pp. 43-84). New York: McGraw-Hill.

Giago, T. (1978). *The aboriginal sin: Reflections on the Holy Rosary Indian Mission School* (Red Cloud Indian School). San Francisco: Indian Historian.

Gibbs, J. C. (1979). The meaning of ecologically oriented inquiry in contemporary psychology. *American Psychologist, 34*, 127-140.

Gibbs, J. C. (1994). Fairness and empathy as the foundation for universal moral education. *Comenius, 14*, 12-23.

Gibbs, J., Potter, G., & Goldstein, A. (1995). *The EQUIP program: Teaching youth to think and act responsibly through peer helping.* Champaign, IL: Research Press.

Gibbs, J., Potter, G., Goldstein, A., & Brendtro, L. (1996). From harassment to helping with antisocial youth: The EQUIP program. *Reclaiming Children and Youth, 5*(1), 40-46.

Gladwell, M. (2002). *The tipping point: How little things can make a big difference.* New York: Little, Brown and Company.

Gold, M. (1995). Charting a course: Promise and prospects for alternative schools. *Journal of Emotional and Behavioural Problems, 3*(4), 8-11.

Gold, M., & Osgood, D. W. (1984). *Expelled to friendlier places.* Ann Arbor: University of Michigan Press.

Gold, M., & Osgood, D. W. (1992). *Personality and peer influence in juvenile corrections.* Westport, CT: Greenwood Press.

Goldstein, A. P. (1993). Interpersonal skills training intervention. In A. P. Goldstein & C. R. Huff (Eds.), *The gang intervention handbook* (pp. 87-157). Champaign, IL: Research Press.

Goldstein, A. P., & Martens, B. K. (2000). *Lasting change: Methods for enhancing generalization of gain.* Champaign, IL: Research Press.

Gottman, J. (2001). *The relationship cure.* New York: Three Rivers Press.

Greenspan, S. I. (1995). *The challenging child.* Reading, MA: Addison-Wesley.

Greenspan, S. I. (1997). *The growth of the mind and the endangered origins of intelligence.* Cambridge, MA: Perseus Books.

Guindon, M. H., Green, A. G., & Hanna, F. J. (2003). Intolerance and psychopathology: Toward a general diagnosis for racism, sexism, and homophobia. *American Journal of Orthopsychiatry, 73*(2), 167-176.

Hadley, M. (Ed.). (2001). *The spiritual roots of restorative justice.* Albany, NY: State University of New York Press.

Hall, S. (1829). *Lectures on school-keeping.* Boston: Richardson, Lord and Holbrook.

Hallowell, E. (2002). Connections. National Adolescent Conference, Scottsdale, Arizona, May 31, 2002. Ben Franklin Institute.

Harlow, H. F. (1958). The nature of love. *American Psychologist, 13,* 673-685.

Healy, W., & Bronner, A. (1936). *New light on delinquency and its treatment.* New Haven, CT: Yale University Press.

Hewitt, J. P. (1998). *The myth of self-esteem.* New York: St. Martin's.

Higgins, G. (1994). *Resilient adults: Overcoming a cruel past.* San Francisco: Jossey-Bass.

Hillman, J. (1996). *The soul's code: In search of character and calling.* New York: Random House.

Hobbs, N. (1994). *The troubled and troubling child.* Cleveland: AREA.

Hoffman, M. L. (1981). Is altruism part of human nature? *Journal of Personality and Social Psychology, 40,* 120-137.

Hubble, M., Duncan, B., & Miller, S. (1999). *The heart and soul of change: What works in therapy.* Washington, DC: American Psychological Association.

Hyman, I. (1997). *School discipline and school violence.* Boston: Allyn and Bacon.

Hyman, I., & Snook, P. (2001). Dangerous schools, alienated students. *Reclaiming Children and Youth, 10*(3), 133-136.

James, W. (1963). Cited in K. Menninger, *The vital balance.* New York: The Viking Press.

Jenkins, R. L., & Brown, W. (1988). *The abandonment of delinquent behaviour.* New York: Praeger.

Johnson, S. (2003). Emotions and the brain. *Discover, 24*(4), 62-69.

Jones, R., & Timbers, G. (2002). An analysis of the restraint event and its behavioural effects on clients and staff. *Reclaiming Children and Youth, 11*(1), 37-41.

Kellerman, J. (1999). *Savage spawn: Reflections on violent children.* New York: Ballantine.

Key, E. (1900). *Barnets Århundrade.* [The Century of the Child]. English edition published in 1909. New York: G. P. Putnam.

Kilpatrick, W. H. (1928). *Education for a changing civilization.* New York: McMillan Company.

Knitzer, J., Steinberg, Z., & Fleisch, B. (1990). *At the schoolhouse door: An examination of programs and policies for children with behavioural and emotional problems.* New York: Bank Street College of Education.

Korczak, J. (1929). *When I am young again* and *The child's right to respect.* Translated by E. P. Kulawic. (1992). Lanham, MD: University Press of America.

Kowalsky, R. M. (1999). Speaking the unspeakable: Self-disclosure and mental health. In R. M. Kowalsky & M. R. Leary (Eds.), *The social psychology of emotional and behaviour problems* (pp. 225-248). Washington, DC: American Psychological Association.

Kozart, M. (2002). Understanding efficacy and psychotherapy: An ethnomethodological perspective on the therapeutic alliance. *American Journal of Orthopsychiatry, 72*(2), 217-231.

Krueger, M. (1998). *Youth work resources.* Washington, DC: CWLA Press.

Kusché, C. A., & Greenberg, M. T. (1994). *The PATHS Curriculum.* Seattle, WA: Developmental Research and Programs.

Lantieri, L., & Patti, J. (1996). *Waging peace in our schools.* Boston: Beacon Press.

Larson, S., & Brendtro, L. (2000). *Reclaiming our prodigal sons and daughters.* Bloomington, IN: National Educational Service.

Lay, J. (2000). The person behind the file number. *Reclaiming Children and Youth, 9*(2), 68-69.

Lazarus, R., & Folkman, S. (1984). *Stress, appraisal, and coping.* New York: Springer.

Leary, M. L. (1999). The social and psychological importance of self esteem. In R. M. Kowalski & M. R. Leary, *The social psychology of emotional and behavioural problems* (pp. 197-221). Washington, DC: American Psychological Association.

LeDoux, J., & Phelps, E. (2000). Emotional networks in the brain. In M. Lewis & J. M. Haviland-Jones (Eds.), *Handbook of Emotions* (2nd ed.) (pp. 157-172). New York: Guilford.

Levy, Z. (1993). *Negotiating positive identity in a group care community: Reclaiming uprooted youth.* New York: Haworth Press.

Lewin, K. (1935). *A dynamic theory of personality. Selected papers.* New York: McGraw.

Lewin, K., Lippit, R., & White, R. K. (1939). Patterns of aggressive behaviour: An experimentally created "social climate." *Journal of Social Psychology, X,* 271-279.

Lickona, T. (2001). What good is character and how can we develop it in our children? *Reclaiming Children and Youth, 9*(4), 239-251.

Liepmann, C. M. (1928). Die selbstventaltung der grefangenen. In C. M. Liepmann, (Ed.), *Hamburgishe Schriften zur Gesamten Strafrechstswessenschaft* (Vol. 12). Berlin: Mannheim.

Long, N. (1995). Why adults strike back. *Reclaiming Children and Youth, 4*(1), 11-15.

Long, N. J. (1997). The therapeutic power of kindness. *Reclaiming Children and Youth, 5*(4), 242-246.

Long, N. J., & Dufner, B. (1980). The stress cycle or the coping cycle: The impact of home and school stresses on pupil's classroom behaviour. In N. J. Long, W. C. Morse, & R. G. Newman (Eds.), *Conflict in the classroom* (4th ed.) (pp. 218-228). Belmont, CA: Wadsworth Publishing Company.

Long, N., Morse, W., & Newman, R. (1997). *Conflict in the classroom.* Austin, TX: PRO-ED.

Long, N., Wood, M., & Fecser, F. (2001). *Life space crisis intervention.* Austin, TX: PRO-ED.

Lynch, J. J. (1977). *The broken heart: The medical consequences of loneliness.* New York: Basic Books.

Machel, G. (2003). Tangible care. In K. Asmal, D. Chidester, & W. James (Eds.), *Nelson Mandela: From freedom to the future.* Johannesburg: Jonathan Ball Publishers,

Maier, H. (1987). *Developmental group care of children.* New York: Haworth Press.

Maslow, A. (1970). *Motivation and personality* (Rev. ed.). New York: Harper & Row.

Mathur, S. R., & Rutherford, R. B. (1996). Is social skills training effective for students with emotional and behavioural disorders? Research issues and needs. *Behavioural Disorders, 22*, 21-28.

Mayer, J., Salovey, P., & Caruso, D. (2000). Models of emotional intelligence. In R. J. Sternberg (Ed.), *The handbook of intelligence* (pp. 396-422). Cambridge, MA: Yale University Press.

McClellan, J. M., & Werry, J. S. (2000). Introduction: Research on psychiatric diagnostic interviews for children and adolescents. *Child and Adolescent Psychiatry, 39*(1), 19-27.

McClellan, J. M., & Werry, J. S. (2004). Evidence-based treatments in child and adolescent psychiatry: An inventory. *Child and Adolescent Psychiatry, 42*(12), 1388-1400.

McCluskey, K., & Mays, A. (2003). *Mentoring for talent development.* Sioux Falls, SD: Reclaiming Youth International.

Mechanic, D. (1978). *Students under stress: A study in the social psychology of adaptation.* Madison, WI: The University of Wisconsin Press.

Meichenbaum, D., & Fong, G. T. (1993). Toward a theoretical model of the role of reasons in nonadherence to health-related advice. In D. M. Wegner & J. W. Pennebaker (Eds.), *Handbook of mental control* (pp. 473-490). Englewood Cliffs, NJ: Prentice-Hall.

Menninger, K. (1959). Hope. *American Journal of Psychiatry, 116,* 481-491.

Menninger, K. (1963). *The vital balance.* New York: The Viking Press.

Milgram, S. (1974). *Obedience to authority.* New York: Harper & Row.

Miller, W., & Rollnick, S. (1991). *Preparing people to change addictive behaviour.* New York: Guilford Press.

Montague, A., & Matson, F. (1979). *The human connection.* New York: McGraw-Hill.

Montaigne, M. (1580). On the education of children. In E. Trechman, (Ed.), *The Essays of Montaigne* (Vol. 1 and 2). (1927). Milford, UK: Oxford University Press.

Montgomery, M. (1997). The powerlessness of punishment: Angry pride and delinquent identity. *Reclaiming Children and Youth, 6*(5), 162-166.

Morse, W. (1985). *The education and treatment of socioemotionally impaired children.* Syracuse, NY: Syracuse University Press.

Mowrer, O. H. (1947). On the dual nature of learning: A reinterpretation of "conditioning" and "problem-solving". *Harvard Educational Review,* 17, 102-148.

Murphy, L. B., & Moriarty, A. E. (1976). *Vulnerability, coping, and growth: From infancy to adolescence.* New Haven, CT: Yale University Press.

Nathanson, D. L. (1992). *Shame and pride: Affect, sex, and the birth of self.* New York: W. W. Norton.

National Film Board of Canada. (1987). *Richard Cardinal: Cry from a diary of a Métis child.* [video]. Montreal, Quebec: Author.

Newkirk, R., & Rutstein, N. (2000). *Racial healing.* Albion, MI: National Resource Centre for the Healing of Racism.

Nichols, P. (2004). No disposable kids: A developmental look at disposability. *Reclaiming Children and Youth, 13*(1), 5-11.

Niebuhr, R. (1932). *Moral man and immoral society: A study in ethics and politics.* New York: Charles Scribner's Sons.

Niehoff, D. (1999). *The biology of violence.* New York: Free Press.

O'Connor, T. G., Rutter, M., & English and Romanian Adoptees Study Team. (2000). Attachment disorder behaviour following early severe deprivation: Extension and longitudinal follow-up. *Child and Adolescent Psychiatry, 39*(6), 703-712.

Odney, J. R., & Brendtro, L. K. (1992). Students grade their schools. *Journal of Emotional and Behavioural Problems, 2*(1), 4-9.

Palmer, P. (1998). *The courage to teach*. San Francisco: Jossey-Bass.

Parese, S. (1999). Understanding the impact of personal crisis on school performance in troubled youth. *Reclaiming Children and Youth, 8*(3), 181-187.

Parks, A. (2002). *An American GULAG: Secret P.O.W. camps for teens*. Eldorado Springs, CO: The Education Exchange.

Paton, A. (1986). *Diepkloof: Reflections of Diepkloof reformatory*. Capetown, South Africa: Credo Press.

Patterson, G. R. (2002a). Future extensions of the models. In J. Reid, G. Patterson, & J. Snyder (Eds.). *Antisocial behaviour in children and adolescents* (pp. 273-283). Washington, DC: American Psychological Association.

Patterson, G. R. (2002b). The early development of coercive family processes. In J. B. Reid, G. Patterson, & J. Snyder (Eds.), *Antisocial behaviour in children and adolescents* (pp. 25-44). Washington, DC: American Psychological Association.

Patterson, G. R., Reid, J., & Eddy, M. (2002). A brief history of the Oregon model. In J. B. Reid, G. Patterson, & J. Snyder (Eds.), *Antisocial behaviour in children and adolescents* (pp. 3-21). Washington, DC: American Psychological Association.

Pennebaker, J. (1990). *Opening up*. New York: Morrow.

Peterson, J. S. (2003). Listening: Resisting the urge to fix them. In K. McCluskey & A. Mays, *Mentoring for talent development* (pp. 126-142). Sioux Falls, SD: Reclaiming Youth International.

Pfister, O. (1956). Therapy and ethics in August Aichhorn's treatment of wayward youth. In K. R. Eisler (Ed.), *Searchlights on delinquency* (pp. 35-49). New York: International Universities Press.

Piaget, J. (1952). *The origins of intelligence in children*. New York: W. W. Norton.

Pilkington, D. (2002). *Rabbit-proof fence*. New York: Miramax Books.

Provine, R. (2000). *Laughter: A scientific investigation*. New York: The Viking Press.

Ramphele, M. (2002). *Steering by the stars: Being young in South Africa*. Cape Town: Tafelberg Publishers.

Rapaport, A. (1960). *Fights, games, and debates*. Ann Arbor, MI: University of Michigan Press.

Raychaba, B. (1993). *Pain, lots of pain: Violence and abuse in the lives of young people in care.* Ottawa, Canada: National Youth in Care Network.

Redl, F. (1957). *When we deal with children.* Glencoe, IL: Free Press.

Redl, F. (1994). The oppositional child and the confronting adult: A mind to mind encounter. In E. James Anthony & Doris G. Gilpin (Eds.), *The clinical faces of childhood* (Vol. 1) (pp. 41-57). Northvale, NJ: Jason Aronson, Inc.

Redl, F., & Wineman, D. (1951). *Children who hate.* Glencoe, IL: Free Press.

Redl, F., & Wineman, D. (1952). *Controls from within.* Glencoe, IL: Free Press.

Redl, F., & Wineman, D. (1957). *The aggressive child.* Glencoe, IL: Free Press.

Reid, J., Patterson, G., & Snyder, J. (Eds.). (2002). *Antisocial behaviour in children and adolescents.* Washington, DC: American Psychological Association.

Reivich, K., & Shatte, A. (2002). *The resilience factor: Seven essential skills for overcoming life's inevitable obstacles.* New York: Broadway Books.

Roberts, M. (2001). *Horse sense for people.* New York: Viking Press.

Roddick, A. (Ed.) (2003). *A revolution in kindness.* West Sussex, UP: Anita Roddick Books.

Rogers, C. (1939). *The clinical treatment of the problem child.* Boston: Houghton Mifflin.

Rosenberg, M. (1999). *Nonviolent communication.* Encinitas, CA: Puddle Dancer Press.

Rotherem-Borus, M. J., & Duan, N. (2003). Next generation of preventive interventions. *Child and Adolescent Psychiatry, 42*(5), 518-526.

Rutter, J. B. (1954). *Social learning and clinical psychology.* Englewood Cliffs, NJ: Prentice Hall.

Rutter, M. (1987). Psychosocial resilience and protective mechanisms. *American Journal of Orthopsychiatry, 57,* 316-331.

Scales, P. C., Benson, P. L., & Roehlkepartain, E. C. (2001). *Grading grown-ups: American adults report on their real relationships with kids.* Minneapolis, MN: Lutheran Brotherhood and Search Institute.

Scheff, T. (1995). Self-Defence against verbal assault: Shame, anger, and the social bond. *Family Process, 34*, 271-286.

Scott, S., McGuire, J., & Shaw, S. (2003). Universal design for instruction. *Remedial and Special Education, 24(6)*, 369-379.

Seita, J., & Brendtro, L. (2004). *Kids who outwit adults.* Bloomington, IN: National Educational Service.

Seita, J., Mitchell, M., & Tobin, C. (1996). *In whose best interest: One child's odyssey, a nation's responsibility.* York, PA: Continental Press.

Seligman, M. (1975). *Helplessness: On depression, development, and death.* San Francisco: W. H. Freeman.

Seligman, M., & Peterson, C. (2003). Positive clinical psychology. In L. G. Aspinwall & U. M. Staudinger (Eds.), *A psychology of human strengths* (pp. 305-318). Washington, DC: American Psychological Association.

Sells, S. (1998). *Treating the tough adolescent.* New York: Guilford Press.

Shores, R., & Wehby, J. (1999). Analyzing the classroom social behaviour of students with EBD. *Journal of Behavioural Disorders, 7(4)*, 194-199.

Shure, M. (1992). *I Can Problem Solve (ICPS): An interpersonal cognitive problem solving program* (preschool, kindergarten-primary, and intermediate grade editions). Champaign, IL: Research Press.

Skinner, B. F. (1948). *Walden II.* New York: Macmillan.

Slaby, A., & Garfinkel, L. (1994). *No one saw my pain.* New York: W. W. Norton.

Solnick, J., Braukmann, C., Bedlington, M., Kirigin, K., & Wolf, M. (1981). The relationship between parent-youth interaction and delinquency in group homes. *Journal of Abnormal Child Psychology, 9(1)*, 107-119.

Sternberg, R. J. (1997). *Successful intelligence.* New York: Plume Books.

Sternberg, R. J. (2000). The concept of intelligence. In R. J. Sternberg (Ed.), *The handbook of intelligence* (pp. 3-15). Cambridge, MA: Yale University Press.

Tangney, J., & Salovey, P. (1999). Problematic social emotions: Shame, guilt, jealousy, and envy. In R. M. Kowalski & M. R. Leary, *The social psychology of emotional and behavioural problems* (pp. 167-195). Washington, DC: American Psychological Association.

Thompson, G., & Jenkins, J. (1993). *Verbal judo: The gentle art of persuasion*. New York: William Morrow.

Tillich, P. (1952). *The courage to be*. New Haven, CT: Yale University Press.

Toch, H., & Adams, K. (2002). *Acting out: Maladaptive behaviour in confinement*. Washington, DC: The American Psychological Association.

Toobey, J., & Cosmides, L. (1990). On the universality of human nature and the uniqueness of the individual. The role of genetics and adaptation. *Journal of Personality, 58,* 17-68.

Toobey, J., & Cosmides, L. (1992). Psychological foundations of culture. In J. Barkow, L. Cosmides, & J. Toobey (Eds.), *The adaptive mind* (pp. 19-136). New York: Oxford University Press.

Torrance, E. P. (1965). *Constructive behaviour*. Belmont, CA: Wadsworth.

Trieschman, A., Whittaker, J., & Brendtro, L. (1969). *The other 23 hours*. New York: Aldine.

Tutu, D. (1997). Cited by M. Battle, *Reconciliation: The ubuntu theology of Desmond Tutu*. Cleveland, OH: Pilgrim Press.

Tutu, D. (2002). Our hope for the future. In L. Brendtro, M. Brokenleg, & S. Van Bockern, *Reclaiming youth at risk* (Rev. ed.). Bloomington, IN: National Educational Service.

Vilakazi, H. (1993). Rediscovering lost truths. *Journal of Emotional and Behavioural Problems, 1*(4), 37.

Villa, D. (1986). The management of misbehaviour by seclusion. *Residential Treatment of Children and Youth, 4*, 63-73.

Viscott, D. (1996). *Emotional resilience*. New York: Crown Publishers.

Vorrath, H. H., & Brendtro, L. K. (1985). *Positive peer culture* (2nd ed.). New York: Aldine de Gruyter.

Vygotsky, L. S. (1989). *Thought and language*. Cambridge, MA: MIT Press.

Wachtel, T. (2003). Restorative justice in everyday life: Beyond the formal ritual. *Reclaiming Children and Youth, 12*(2), 83-87.

Waller, J. (2002). *Becoming evil: How ordinary people commit genocide and mass killing*. New York: Oxford University Press.

Wallin, B. (1994). *Giving the boot to boot camps*. Master's Thesis, Augustana College, Sioux Falls, SD.

Walsh, F. (1998). *Strengthening family resilience*. New York: Guilford Press.

Wasmund, W., & Tate, T. (1996). *Partners in empowerment: A peer group primer.* Albion, MI: Starr Commonwealth.

Werner, E. (1995). Resilience and development. *American Psychological Society, 4,* 81-85.

Werner, E., & Smith, R. (1992). *Overcoming the odds: High risk children from birth to adulthood.* Ithaca, NY: Cornell University Press.

Whalen, R., & Kauffman, J. (1999). *Educating children with emotional and behavioural disorders.* Reston, VA: Council for Exceptional Children.

White, M. (1995). *Re-authoring lives.* Adelaide, Australia: Dulwich Centre Publications.

White, M., & Epston, D. (1990). *Narrative means to therapeutic ends.* New York: W. W. Norton.

White, R. (1959). Motivation reconsidered: The concept of competence. *Psychological Review, 66,* 297-313.

Wilker, K. (1920). *Der Lindenhof.* Translated 1993 by Stephan Lhotzky. Sioux Falls, SD: Augustana College.

Willner, A., Braukmann, C., Kirigin, K., Fixsen, D., Phillips, E., & Wolf, M. (1970). The training and validation of youth-preferred social behaviours of child-care personnel. *Journal of Applied Behaviour Analysis, 10*(2), 219-230.

Wolin, S., & Wolin, S. (1993). *The resilient self.* New York: Villard.

Winnicott, D. (1965). *The maturational process and the facilitating environment: Studies in the theory of emotional development.* New York: International Universities Press.

Wood, F. H. (1988). Factors in intervention choice. *Monograph in Behavioural Disorders, 11,*133-143. Arizona State University and Council for Children with Behavioural Disorders.

Yalom, I. (1995). *The theory and practice of group psychotherapy* (4th ed.). New York: Basic Books.

Zehr, H. (2002). *The little book of restorative justice.* Intercourse, PA: Good Books.

Zeigarnik, B. (1927). Das Behalten von erledigten und unerledigten Handlungen (The memory of completed and uncompleted tasks). *Psychologische Forschung, 9,* 1-85.

Zillmann, D. (1993). Mental control of angry aggression. In D. Wegner & J. Pennebaker (Eds.), *Handbook of mental control* (pp. 370-392). Upper Saddle River, NJ: Prentice-Hall.

Zinbardo, P. G., Maslach, C., & Haney, C. (2000). Reflections on the Stanford prison experiment: Genesis, transformations, consequences. In T. Blass (Ed.), *Obedience to authority: Current perspectives on the Milgram paradigm* (pp. 193-237). Mahwah, NJ: Erlbaum.

Art Credits

p. x   **Silenced**; Rebecca Kirby, National Association of Homes and Services for Children youth art contest winner

p. xii   **Self-portrait** by unidentified Canadian youth from the National Youth In Care Network of Canada

p. 6   **Boy banging head into wall**; Justin Nordmeyer, age 15, Oak Park, Illinois

p. 9   **Angry teddy bear**; Justin Nordmeyer, age 15, Oak Park, Illinois

p. 13   **The Circle of Courage**; George Blue Bird, Sioux Falls, South Dakota

p. 15   **Heart in a Vise**, Denisha, age 17, Duluth, Minnesota

p. 16   **Kids behind bars**; Angie Larson, Augustana College, Sioux Falls, South Dakota

p. 19   **"I am locked away"**; Eli, age 19, Sioux Falls, South Dakota

p. 25   **Self-portrait of an abused girl**; Anna Caroline Jennings

p. 36   **Australia Alive**; Shaun, age 18, Perth, Australia

p. 52   **Peace and Harmony**; Jay, Lawrence Hall Youth Services, Chicago, Illinois

p. 55   **Self-portrait**; Erin, age 17, Brandon, South Dakota

p. 64   **Child in pain**; Art from the publication *Bruise*, written and illustrated by the children of Hannah Neil, Columbus, Ohio

RAP Training Resources

Response Ability Pathways – or simply RAP – is a training program providing skills for working effectively with children and youth, supporting them on pathways toward responsibility. RAP training is highly practical and can be provided both to mentors and mature youth. RAP builds positive connections among youth and with their elders and creates climates of mutual respect.

Problems as Opportunities

To succeed in the face of risk and challenge, children need concerned adults and peers who respond to their needs rather than react to problem behaviour. RAP provides these "response-abilities" to all who deal directly with young persons experiencing conflict in school, family, peer group, and community. This training can include key adult stakeholders as well as youth who exercise positive influence among their peers.

RAP is a system for communicating with youth and providing positive support. RAP uses a clear-cut problem-solving format: *Connect > Clarify > Restore.* This is the normal process for resilient coping found in all cultures. Thus, RAP taps the strengths and natural capacity kids already have to *connect* with others for support, *clarify* challenging problems, and *restore* respect. Problems become positive learning opportunities.

RAP starts with problems but searches for strengths and solutions. RAP provides whatever support the "teaching moment" allows, whether literally a moment or an hour. Sometimes a few short RAP interventions distributed over time have more lasting impact than a long session.

RAP training grew from the Circle of Courage model based on Native American philosophies of child rearing as described in *Reclaiming Youth At Risk* by Larry Brendtro, Martin Brokenleg, and Steve Van Bockern. The goal is to create opportunities for belonging, mastery, independence, and generosity. RAP is also grounded in research on resilience and brain science.

RAP training has been rated as highly useful by staff in education, treatment, juvenile justice, youth care, foster care, family support, law enforcement, and community and faith-based organizations. RAP enables youth to join in an alliance with adults to solve problems and cultivate respectful environments.

Course Content of RAP Training

I. RAP Foundations
- Foundational Concepts
- Circle of Courage and Resilience Science
- Rivers of Pain
- Fighting Pain with Pain

II. Connecting
- RAP Introduction
- Disconnected Kids
- Brain Science on Connecting
- Strategies for Connecting

III. Clarifying
- Coping With Challenges
- Private Logic: The Inside Kid
- Thinking Errors
- CLEAR Thinking

IV. Restoring
- Instiling Responsibility
- Cultivating Respect
- Restoring Social Bonds
- Choosing New Pathways

Organization of RAP Training

RAP training follows principles of "universal design." It is intuitive, jargon-free, and relevant across diverse cultural settings. Training is interactive and experiential and provides practical strategies for professional and lay persons as well as youth who are peer leaders. A RAP course is delivered over three or four days by certified RAP trainers. Participants in RAP workshops can register to receive undergraduate or graduate credit or Continued Professional Development [CPD] points.

Skills for the RAP process are developed in sequence, first

concentrating on Connecting, then adding Clarifying, and by the last day putting together Connecting, Clarifying, and Restoring. Videos and role plays capture real-life challenges and provide essential skills for success with challenging children and youth. The RAP text supports formal training activities.

Research Foundations of RAP

RAP uses a philosophy of restorative intervention grounded in two major bodies of research. First, the Circle of Courage translates the mushrooming literature on resilience and positive youth development into a concise and understandable format. Secondly, RAP is an application of recent brain research in areas such as conflict, emotional intelligence, and pain-based behaviour. RAP translates this knowledge into practical strategies for connecting with youth at risk, creatively solving problems, and fostering pro-social behaviour.

Arranging RAP Training

RAP training can be customised to particular needs of a group or organization. For further information about opportunities for RAP training, contact:

Child & Youth Care Agency for Development [CYCAD]
P. O. Box 12036
Hatfield, Pretoria
0028 South Africa
E-mail info@cycad.org.za

No Disposable Kids
Starr Commonwealth Road
Albion, MI 49224-9580
E-mail dobbinsm@starr.org

Circle of Courage
P.O. Box 57
Lennox, SD 57039 USA
E-mail courage@reclaiming.com

About the Authors

Larry K. Brendtro is former president of Starr Commonwealth in Michigan and Ohio. He holds a Ph.D. in the combined program in education and psychology from the University of Michigan specializing in troubled children and youth. He founded the nonprofit organization Reclaiming Youth international and is senior editor of the journal *Reclaiming Children and Youth.* He has many years of experience as a child and youth care worker, educator, psychologist, and program executive. Larry has been a professor of special education in the field of behavior disorders at the University of Illinois, The Ohio State University, and Augustana College. He is currently a member of the adjunct graduate faculty of the School of Child and Youth Care at the University of Victoria in British Columbia, Canada. He has authored over a hundred articles and currently has ten books in print. Larry Brendtro, Martin Brokenleg, and Steve Van Bockern developed the Circle of Courage model of positive youth development and have provided training in twenty nations and in dozens of indigenous cultures worldwide. Dr. Brendtro is an adopted member of the Rosebud Lakota tribe and divides his time between the Black Hills of South Dakota and Starr Commonwealth in Michigan.

Lesley du Toit is executive director of the Child and Youth Care Agency for Development [CYCAD] in South Africa which serves orphans and vulnerable children in rural areas and provides training and consultation to government and non-profit organizations. She is former director of the National Association of Child Care Workers in South Africa. During the administration of President Nelson Mandela, she was chosen by Minister Geraldine Fraser-Moleketi to manage the transformation of the child and youth care system through the Inter-ministerial Committee on Children and Youth at Risk. She has extensive experience in child and youth care and social work, having worked in residential care and community programs. She earned an honors degree in social work, and holds a masters degree in child care administration from Nova University. She was instrumental in establishing the first graduate degree program for child and youth care professionals in South Africa and has served as a lecturer at the University of South Africa in Pretoria. She has addressed youth professionals throughout South Africa and in Europe and North America. Recently, she has been appointed as Deputy Minister of the Department of Children and Family Development for British Columbia. Lesley is an adopted member of the Batlokwa Sotho Tribal Council, representing a mountain kingdom in Qwa Qwa, Free State. She is currently living in Victoria, British Columbia, Canada.